Eden's Legacy

Gabriel Deeds

Trafford Publishing

© Copyright 2004 Gabriel Deeds. All rights reserved.

No part of this publication may be reproduced, stored in a retrieval system, or transmitted, in any form or by any means, electronic, mechanical, photocopying, recording, or otherwise, without the written prior permission of the author.

Printed in Victoria, Canada

Note for Librarians: a cataloguing record for this book that includes Dewey Classification and US Library of Congress numbers is available from the National Library of Canada. The complete cataloguing record can be obtained from the National Library's online database at:
www.nlc-bnc.ca/amicus/index-e.html

ISBN 1-4120-1737-8

TRAFFORD

This book was published on-demand in cooperation with Trafford Publishing.
On-demand publishing is a unique process and service of making a book available for retail sale to the public taking advantage of on-demand manufacturing and Internet marketing. On-demand publishing includes promotions, retail sales, manufacturing, order fulfilment, accounting and collecting royalties on behalf of the author.

Suite 6E, 2333 Government St., Victoria, B.C. V8T 4P4, CANADA
Phone   250-383-6864   Toll-free 1-888-232-4444 (Canada & US)
Fax   250-383-6804   E-mail sales@trafford.com
Web site www.trafford.com   TRAFFORD PUBLISHING IS A DIVISION OF TRAFFORD HOLDINGS LTD.
Trafford Catalogue #03-2114   www.trafford.com/robots/03-2114.html
  10   9   8   7   6   5   4   3   2

Acknowledgements

To my Dad, for a life that wasn't wasted

To my Mum who has always been there.

Thanks to my Mother and Sister who understood and even when they didn't understand, didn't try to stop me. Thanks to Teresa who was the first to read Eden's Legacy and helped me get over the panic.

The Author

David McCaughey, pen name Gabriel Deeds, was born in Tanzania, June 4, 1960 at the Williamson diamond mine, the only hospital around. Both his Mother and his Father are Irish, his Mother from Wexford and his Father from Antrim. He has travelled the world extensively and now lives part of the year in the English Lake District and part of the year in Vancouver, Canada.

He left a career in local government to take up writing full time. Eden's Legacy is his first book. He is now working on a thriller, The Minstrel Boy, and a series of children's stories, Piccolo the Panther.

www.bolddeeds.co.uk

www.edenslegacy.com

The Swastika

卐   卐

The Swastika has been around for thousands of years, long before a certain ambitious Austrian tried to corrupt it. Even then he deliberately chose the left handed Swastika which, some believe, represents the dark side. The Swastika originally represented life and the revolving sun, the sign of a benevolent Universe. This was indicated by the right hand or clockwise revolution as above, whilst the left handed or counter clockwise Swastika below represented the opposite. The word is derived from Sanskrit where it means conducive to well being. Uniquely it is used in all the major religions of the world regardless of geography.

China, Tibet, Japan, India, Persia and all the countries of the East have been using the Swastika as a religious symbol for Good going back ten thousand years. The South American Mayans and the North American Indians also used it extensively. The ancient Mesopotamian people and the early Christians used it and in Byzantium it was used on coins and in art. In Russia and Scandinavia and all over Europe the Swastika was well known as a symbol of fertility and good luck.

The Swastika is common to all the major religions and I have chosen it to represent the concept of a Universal Consciousness that unites us all. The choice of Good or Evil is a personal choice, your personal choice.

Gabriel Deeds

Structure and contents

Introduction

Chapters 1-5 What the hell happened to you!

Chapter One : The road to hell
Chapter Two: Life and Death
Chapter Three : Younique
Chapter Four: Born into Conflict
Chapter Five: Self confidence

Chapter 6-8 Personal Audit, where am I?

Chapter Six: The secret being
Chapter Seven: What do you believe?
Chapter Eight: Success, a new definition

Chapters 9-15 Offence and defence- counter measures.

Chapter Nine: Offence
Chapter Ten: Assertion skills
Chapter Eleven: Self Defence
Chapter Twelve: Social Interaction, surviving it!
Chapter Thirteen: The Body
Chapter Fourteen: The Mind
Chapter Fifteen: The Action Plan

Chapter Sixteen: Conclusion

Epilogue

Appendices

EDEN'S LEGACY

Sentient: – Self aware, conscious of one's place in the Universe.

Introduction

We spend much of our short lives avoiding the truth. The truth of our own Self awareness and the responsibilities that being a sentient being bring. Some of us are truly ignorant, never actually attaining any degree of sentience. They, we, fail miserably to achieve our own potential dying unfulfilled in the darkness.

Millions of us bound in the daily struggle for survival may lack the opportunity. Those poor souls at the mercy of war, famine, disease and poverty. I do not refer to the stressed Teacher or the overworked office worker. Although we may feel that we lack the opportunity in fact it is merely that we choose to avoid it. Instead we choose to spend our lives evading the dread questions of our own existence, why are we here? What is the point?

Sentience or Self awareness is a great gift, a rare opportunity for the development of the individual thus blessed and for the advancement of all. It is Eden's Legacy. Why then do we fear it so? Why do we hide from it and waste the most precious aspect of our lives?

The answers, some of them, are in this book, as they are in many books and television and on the Internet. You will find suggested movies and web sites throughout the book. I feel your sadness, your unease and discontent for they belong to me as well, but what do we do about it? Our pain must teach us if we are to have any peace at all. Let us suffer for a purpose.

Use your God given intelligence to solve your own life's dilemma. Stop running, turn and stand you're ground, you can't hide from God and you can't hide from your Self. What choice do you really have? You can live like any other primate till the day you die, or, you can become what you are and realise your own personal potential.

My beliefs leak into this book, that I cannot help, but primarily this book is about you and what you believe and how you live your life. It is about our natural Spirituality, not religion. Ultimately, we are Spiritual beings in denial. I will often refer to Salvation, Enlightenment and personal fulfilment. I believe these terms to be completely interchangeable. I say again, religion comes a very distant second to Spirituality.

Eden's Legacy is designed to try to focus and define the intangible nature of our responsibility to ourselves and to others. It sets objectives and lays out a structured plan to enable us to begin to search for our own fulfilment. The book is divided into the three sections on page five.

Section one, what has happened to you.
Section two, your current status.
Section three, defence and offence.

Please orientate yourself so that you know where you are in the book at all times, this can be a complex and confusing subject. The book is also interactive in that there are tasks for you to perform as you read. Please complete them as you come to them.

There is an old proverb,

"You can lead a horse to water, but you cannot make it drink."

Humanity is standing by the water trough, parched, desperate to drink and yet it seems we would rather die.

In the words of Christ and Buddha,

"Seek and ye shall find."

"Diligently seek your own Salvation."

Drink, begin the adventure that is your life.

Section One

Chapters 1-5   What the hell happened to you!

Chapter One : The road to hell

1. The Hive
2. Evolution
3. Hell on earth

Chapter Two: Life and Death

1. Your Life
2. Your Death
3. Super being or zombie

Chapter Three : Younique

1. Opportunity
2. The Catch
3. Be selfish

Chapter Four: Born into Conflict

1. You verses Them
2. Other people's expectations
3. You are the key

Chapter Five: Self confidence

1. The cycle
2. How and why it is taken from us
3. Victim and assailant

Gabriel Deeds

Chapter 1   The Road to Hell

I believe that we are taught to fear that which we do not understand. We do not understand our own existence, the essence of Self, therefore we fear it. We avoid it like the plague and yet it haunts us, it fascinates us. Of course it does, what could be more interesting to the individual than itself? How could we possibly hide from ourselves? Why would we want to?

Although we have the intelligence to understand we do not begin the analysis because it is difficult and because we learn from a very early age that our lives are expected to conform to a rigid set of rules and parameters. The needs of the many outweigh the needs of the few and of the one

These rules are imposed on us by our biological conditioning and the culture in which we live. This is well before we become Self aware, whilst we are still reliant and compliant. These narrow boundaries are policed by our parents, families, peers, the people that we associate with, our tribe. By a society which has already largely failed to appreciate or even notice Self. I call this coalition the Hive and will often refer to it in the following pages.

Its greatest manifestation is how it shapes your thoughts and the thoughts of those around you and therefore your actions. Ironically, it is powerless without you. It only exists in you and those around you. Its principal tools are fear and conflict with which it moulds the evolutionary power that has largely shaped us, survival of the fittest. There exists then, a most damaging conflict between Self and society. The individual verses the Hive.

Exploration of Self is daunting, even terrifying, but it is also deeply discouraged by our society, which advocates the promotion of Self sacrifice for the good of the community. This is in fact nothing more than an animal instinct, an evolutionary strategy to elevate us to the top of the food chain. The pack is more powerful than the individual. A very successful strategy, but we are more than just another species, we are Self aware.

" The needs of the many outweigh the needs of the few and of the one."

A seemingly noble sentiment, one that has led us to despair! It seems to eschew the ideals of Self sacrifice but in fact the Hive has corrupted the ideal and made it a tool for Self suppression. If the basic building block of society, the individual, is fractured and confused, how can it be used to build anything good? The "many", society, merely magnifies and reflects the suffering of the individual. You cannot sacrifice Self until you have understood and possessed it.

Only when you have realised the value of Self does it become a fitting and necessary sacrifice.

If we are to evolve further and avoid destruction or decimation through over population, we must rise above our own cycle of biological evolution. First a few individuals must succeed spreading the acceptance of Self. Then the powers that be must recognise the value and the necessity of this valuable resource.

Until society accepts the fact that the individual Self is the fundamental building block upon which we build our future we will always be victims of our own biological success. Like rabbits we will be controlled by Mother Nature through famine, drought, pestilence and war. In our blind struggle for survival we will destroy or be destroyed until we are cast aside for a species with more potential.

It is not enough for a few individuals to succeed, there must be a fundamental shift in the way we think. We like to think of ourselves as the only sentient species on the planet but we don't do much thinking at all. Reflection i.e. careful thought, should be the precursor to our actions. Somehow we have managed to turn this precept on it's head, we react before we reflect. Thought itself has become merely a reaction to events. Every individual must be encouraged and taught to think without fear of the consequences. Only then can we bring to bear our greatest weapon, our own natural intelligence and innate Spirituality. We must all individually and collectively seek our own Enlightenment.

To achieve this objective our strategy must be the classic pincer movement. On the one flank, our own personal Salvation, and on the other, the flowering of compassion for all who suffer as we do. To hope that each adult will somehow manage to realise their own potential is foolish. We are too damaged. Our destiny is to step forward into the reeking breach of ignorance, fear and intolerance and to fight for change. Those that follow will climb over us and beyond. It is our destiny to be the catalyst, the blue touch paper, that starts a chain reaction that will ultimately elevate the Human race to its rightful place.

Ironically, Self sacrifice is the only route to Salvation or personal fulfilment.

This flowering of compassion must be especially evident in the education of our children. After all, we love them, we cherish them, don't we? The term education must be re-defined to incorporate a more rounded in depth curriculum that reflects this new thinking. Resources must then be applied lavishly, outside geography and politics, in a way that has not been seen before. On a par for example with what we spend on nuclear deterrents and star wars technology. Every child should be treated as the saviour of the Human race. That is exactly what they are!

Every pot bellied, starving urchin that dies of disease or starvation is a priceless treasure lost and a damning indictment of our species. Every truant child that is bullied in the playground or excluded from school for bullying is another tragedy, another millstone around our necks. They, stagger into the world, the survivors, under the burden we have placed on their tiny shoulders. How can they thrive and prosper? How can we? For remember, they are us. We must seek to save ourselves so that we can save them and break the cycle of suffering.

Within human society, as in the playground, there is an undermining intolerance of any deviation from the accepted norm. Such deviations inherently imply criticism of the ruling system. More implicitly it highlights the weakness of those who have already accepted the system.

Again, this intolerance is in large measure a biological trait. All primates depend heavily on the social cohesion of the community they live in. Differences in behaviour, thinking or even physical appearance, anything outside the norm are expurgated ruthlessly without thought. Unless it is strong enough to endure and overcome.

Children are well known for being cruel to other children who may have a different accent or be particularly shy or just unusual. Consequently they learn quickly to mimic and conform to the group norms. This learned behaviour is habit forming and addictive. To this day my blood runs cold when I hear the sound of children chanting in the playground around a pair of fighting youngsters,

"Col-in, Col-in, Col-in." Such willing students, such enthusiasm for the subject. Each child constantly monitoring the reactions of those around, hiding and comparing Each child secretly relieved that it is not them, secretly afraid of being next. Which one of them will say?

" Stop it, let him up, leave him alone?" Why none of course, they are children, they do what we teach them and what their animal instincts dictate. Which of us would come forward in a similar situation?

Taken a step further there is also a tendency to attack as a means of drawing the group's attention away from the attacker to the victim. This is a dominant form of behaviour and nurtures a deep seated desire for approval from the peer group at the expense of Self. Then there is the comedian, desperately trying to deflect the pack with pathetic humour. Even as I write my eyes fill with tears, who among us has not endured this suffering? We want to belong. At this critical, tender age we learn to camouflage Self in multitudinous ways and develop an outer distorted projection of ourselves. Here then is the mutilated seedling that will be crippled until the day it dies.

This is learned behaviour, not completely instinctive, and as we grow older so we progress in the dark arts of intolerance, criticism, manipulation, and bigotry. From the playground to the boardroom, to countless mass graves and slave camps. This tendency to follow the mob at the expense of Self, led us to the Third Reich, Communism, Capitalism, from one Empire to another, it led us to the crucifixion of Christ. We are all enslaved by fear. Fear of our peers, of being different, of ourselves.

Tremendous, insidious and unwavering pressure is brought to bear on those who dare to be different. Many therefore fall by the wayside and join the obedient, dumb ranks of bovine drones. Or worse they waste their whole lives in the stultifying stupor of the Hive. It is they who are especially unforgiving of any future questioning that may open old wounds and expose their weakness.

In their subconscious Self loathing and guilt is a vicious desire to destroy anything that reminds them of the Self they have turned their backs on. Incredible strength and resolve is required to endure this unrelenting attack.

Few have that strength, but from those few must come the many and finally the all. Our evolution must make a quantum leap from the biological to the Spiritual or humanity will exercise it's own freedom to destroy itself.

How can we achieve anything other than our own propagation if we do not value the individual, if we do not study and cherish ourselves? A society of Self possessed, open minded individuals would value the questioning process. A society of Self repressed, Self loathing cynics would fight it tooth and nail. It is this basic conflict, which leads us to fill our lives with illusion and Self deceit, and prevents us from addressing a problem, which we are well able to tackle if we will only allow ourselves.

Modern living, commonly referred to as the rat race, is a deeply unsatisfying, corrosive, miserable experience. It leads us into unfulfilling careers, tortuous relationships and bad health, both physical and mental.

In extreme cases we are driven to Self destruction through alcohol and drugs or just plain old suicide. No other known species will actually make a conscious decision to take its own life rather than endure the pain of an unfulfilled, pointless existence. (Fight Club, appendix 2). It is acceptable, even admirable, in some quarters to achieve freedom from our consciousness in huge amounts of alcohol and mindless debauchery. (Hurly Burly, appendix 2).

It has become an industry, Club 18-30, Falaraki, the Mediterranean coast of Greece and Spain. Young people without beliefs or understanding, like lost tormented souls squirming in agony. Friday night becomes the only reason for enduring the existence of the drone within the Hive.

Then there is retail therapy, an all too common phenomenon, the sad trawling through piles of glittering trash and the mad scramble to expend valuable resources on gear which we do not need or really want. There is the desperate industry of the DIY fiend and again the inveterate gardener.

Two of the most common deceptions we use to distract ourselves are that pillar of our society, the Work Ethic, and the search for El Dorado, love. More people use these distractions than perhaps any other.

Eden's Legacy

The work ethic, duty, is seen as an admirable quality engendered into us from birth, sometimes at the expense of our lives. (Remains Of The Day, appendix 2). Here we can find status, respect and more importantly, oblivion. We can indefinitely and comfortably avoid anything of substance in our lives until the day we die.

The search for love leads us to lust, relationships, partnership, marriage, families, divorce and so on and so on. Combined with work, an admirable means of suppressing Self. To dream of "True Love" is to undermine Self. It is to believe that Self is not enough, unacceptable, insufficiently important. To believe that we must latch onto someone else to be enough, to keep society happy is to deny completely the value of Self. That is not to say that true love cannot exist, it can, but not before Self. More on theses two later in the book.

More mundane but just as pathetic is the hair shirt of charitable works, civic duty or for the truly incorrigible, politics. We even use our own families as a distraction putting everything into rearing the children only to find our lives empty when they leave.

There is nothing inherently wrong with any of the above activities; it is just that we often use them to avoid the reality of our responsibilities. We are not just another species content to beaver away unthinking. We must be more than that. Until we have mastered ourselves or are at least studying Self we can be of no use to anyone else and our species will ultimately perish.

Life can seem interminable when it is empty. We vainly try to fill it with distractions and yet ultimately, especially for those full of regrets, it is but a moment. Your life is a finite resource, it will end, of that you can be certain. It doesn't matter how old you are, it matters only that you begin to peel away the layers of Self deceit and illusion and get to know and love your true Self.

Sometimes it is only towards the end that realisation dawns. Ironically we are all familiar with the near death experience that changes someone's life. The car smash, the heart bypass, the brush with cancer. We are all familiar with the experience. It usually washes over us in a moment of titillation as we read about it or hear about it in the pub.

" Brain haemorrhage, 41 and fell into his muesli at the breakfast table!"

Gabriel Deeds

We hear but we do not listen. Why is it, that as supposedly the only sentient species on this planet, we suffer such torment? Why do we fail to learn from the accumulated wisdom, which surrounds us? Why do we repeat the same mistakes over and over again? Even our own experiences can be ignored or fail to have any lasting impact. We seem to have an incredible ability to avoid the responsibility of our own sentient consciousness.

Yet it gnaws us, it hounds us, even in our subconscious it follows unceasing, it will never release us. It is this legacy we hide from, Eden's Legacy. Since we first tasted the apple from the tree of Knowledge we have fled from God and ourselves. In hiding we create our own suffering through our fear and Self imposed ignorance. In trying to avoid the inevitable we create our own living hell.

Resources, see also appendix 1 and 2.

Books – How To practice: the way to a meaningful life.
Movies - American Beauty, Matrix.

Chapter 2   Life and Death

When you were born, when any child is born it should be a cause for celebration and joy. We are filled with wonder at the miracle of new life, a life so innocent, so bright, so full of hope and potential. For a brief time we forget the accumulated baggage of our own damaged lives and revel in that simple joy, a child.

We love to watch our children sleeping in peaceful, careless, contentment. We watch in wonder full of gentle envy, mindful of what we have lost.

Then, shaking ourselves from our romantic idyll, we begin the serious work of adapting the child so that she can survive in our world of real life fantasy. Instead of changing the world and God knows it needs changing, we strive to change the child. Now the child is already as perfect as any of us can ever hope to be! So what do we think we are doing? Well, we don't "think" about it much at all.

Babies are like blank sheets of paper or photographic film. To realise their potential life must leave its mark. They are equally susceptible to positive or negative influences. The finished product is the most important thing in the world, it is something that we and society should daily struggle to improve and perfect.

When we think of baby it is easy to strive to do our best to equip them for life. Long hours at work, private education, toys, blah, blah, blah. They become an excuse to help us forget the other baby in our own lives, the one that perhaps is not as adorable and easy to make sacrifices for. You. We fail to recognise the value of Self and so we fail to pass on the concept to our children. We fail the children and we fail ourselves. We merely perpetuate the cycle. We must both save ourselves and holistically educate our children if we are to break the cycle and evolve.

As cycles go our own life cycle is perhaps the most important and yet it is also the one that we constantly overlook. In everyday living we become buried in the mundane routine and what can seem like the crushing burden of making ends meet. We get up, we go to work, we eat we sleep. Holidays to save for, bills to pay, ambitions to fulfil. That bigger house, the new car, a better office with more power. This is how you were raised, what your parents wanted for you, what society expects. This is how we think, how we measure ourselves, we are like racehorses pulling milk carts.

We would argue that we are doing our best for our family. In actual fact most of the time we are just reacting to situations and the expectations of our peers rather than making conscious life decisions. It is easier to be busy than to think, we prefer to be busy fools.

We are expected to do certain things and behave in certain ways. As children we are greatly influenced by the adults around us. We pick up their ways and habits, we copy them. As children we are not fully aware, we are not strong enough to understand. Our sentience grows, our consciousness evolves and we are constantly at loggerheads with our peers.

It is during these years that the forming sentient can be empowered or crippled, more commonly it is a mixture of the two. This process is as important to the parent and society as it is to the child. No system should be blindly accepted, unchallenged for that is how vicious circles begin. Look at our schools today, huge factories for processing children. Glorified day care for working parents. They have become hostels for swarms of damaged souls who in their turn blindly go forth and multiply. Of course this is a generalisation, but why should our children's education be a matter of luck or resources? Why is the holistic education of our children not a priority?

It is very simple, we cannot teach that which we do not know.

This process of growing up is commonly regarded as a conflict and all too often because we do not consciously reflect on what is happening we use crushing force to control what can be regarded as a nuisance, our own children. The child's independent Self poses serious threats to the stability of our own comfortable illusions and the very fabric of our society. This is a good thing! The tragedy is that we teach the child to suppress Self and adapt to our warped sense of how things should be. We create conflict and fear and convince our children that this is how the world is. This horrible world shapes our children with our help, even with our blessing.

We teach that Self is selfish, that we are members of family, community, society. There are rules, we cannot say or do what we think, we must make sacrifices and compromise to be good citizens and to survive. Self is bad, it must be suppressed, disciplined, excised.

I would argue that if we look out for our own "Self" and are aware of our own value to the Universe we are in a much stronger position to positively affect those around us. A strong Self also makes us aware of our responsibilities to other people and their development. We would quickly realise that we are in fact completely interdependent. If each of us did no more than concentrate on saving ourselves, achieving Heaven or Enlightenment or whatever you want to call it, what a different world we would live in.

If we are brainwashed into living as our peers would wish us to, there is a strong chance that none of this will come to light. If it does surface it is a source of considerable confusion and much psychotherapy, if we are fortunate. If we are unfortunate it can lead to a tortuous life, to isolation and to misery. We often retreat into our old comfortable world of illusion throwing ourselves into one of the aforementioned life styles. Our Self is then suppressed and we suffer the blight of unfulfilled living torment.

A cycle that is not studied and understood can become a vicious circle. All of us fall victim to this deadly trap. It is necessary first to recognise what has happened to you and then to break out of the cycle.

If we take the baby as the start of the cycle what chance does she have if you, her parent, are part of the vicious circle?

She will find herself in the same situation that you find your Self in now. As an individual she may have a better or worse chance of sorting out her life, in fact she should benefit from your experience. Her chances should be far better as a result of your suffering, not worse. We tend to pass on our conditioning rather than teach our children and emphasise the incredible value of the individual and the opportunity that sentient birth presents.

Since we do not take the time to understand what has happened to us and learn from our experience our children are doomed to repeat our mistakes. It is much more difficult, often impossible, to repair damaged adults! Ten thousand times better to nurture and teach our children and break the cycle that unchecked will one day destroy our species.

Gabriel Deeds

Talk is cheap, how do we begin? We begin in the only way we can, with ourselves. This is one battle we can fight and win. We must at the very least begin to fight for ourselves and future generations if the cycle is to be broken. Our children cannot save themselves, we must show them the way but first we must save ourselves.

Objectivity is the key to success here. It is very hard to achieve objectivity when so much of what we believe about ourselves is Self deceit. Remember too that before you can improve your lot you must honestly recognise how bad things are. This is not a negative thing although it may feel like it.

This is perhaps the most compelling reason for avoiding Self scrutiny in the first place. After years of evading the truth you cannot expect to suddenly find that your fur lined rut, that enveloping womb of deception, is miraculously a deeply satisfying place. It is merely a projection, a shield, a prison cell. You have work to do.

Like the hermit crab, ultimately you will outgrow your shell and must move on, cast it off. It offers no real protection, only a temporary respite from reality, which inevitably becomes a deadly constricting trap.

Recognising it is a deep shock that leaves you suddenly exposed and vulnerable. After years in his cage the budgie realises the door is open, his freedom is at hand, his life's dream is about to be realised. He hops onto the doorstep and looks out. The freedom he has sought is now available, he cannot blame the cage, now is his time to fly.

"Who will feed me? Where will I go? What is out there?"

Iron bars do not a prison make, the budgie stays in his cage. The only thing that has changed is that now, he knows, deep in his subconscious that he is a coward. Now he despises himself.

If you begin this journey you will certainly try to return to your comfortable illusion when the pressure is on. It's seductive allure, it's subtle, insidious cunning will deceive you into error. This is inevitable, so prepare for victory and defeat, remain steadfast in both, do not be distracted by either. One is as dangerous as the other. You will fall in love, you might be promoted at work, you will tell your Self that things aren't so bad. You must be constantly vigilant.

There is only the fight, there is no winning or losing. Focus on this alone. Do not expect to win great victories or suffer crushing defeats, in those famous words from Kipling's "If", (see appendix 1),

Eden's Legacy

> If you can meet with Triumph and Disaster
>
> And treat those two impostors just the same

When you are suffering be kind to your Self, when you are happy be cautious. Constant vigilance is necessary for you will never completely expunge your conditioning, the illusion that was your life, from your soul. It will be your implacable enemy to the end of your days. Remember it is ultimately the root of all your troubles and woes.

In many ways it has been unwittingly perpetrated on you through your own family and upbringing in a society that cares little for the individual. You must be good to your Self, hold your Self in high esteem, for there is no higher goal, no more difficult quest than the understanding of your own true Self. You will be shocked, horrified even, at the depth and complexity of the multi-layered smothering shell that has been built around you. It is a true prison in which your soul pines for freedom.

It is the rare person who can ask themselves the big questions and be satisfied with the answer. Give your Self credit for being honest enough and strong enough to even attempt to face up to the Truth. Low Self esteem is a dreadfully common side effect of modern upbringing and must be systematically rooted out as far as possible. There is more on how to combat it further on in the book, for now, recognise your Self as a valiant soul, get to like your Self.

Here are some words of wisdom that might help.

"Our deepest fear is not that we are inadequate; our deepest fear is that we are powerful beyond measure. It is our light, not our darkness that most frightens us. We ask ourselves who am I to be gorgeous, talented and fabulous? Actually who are you not to be? You are a child of God. Your playing small doesn't serve the world. There is nothing enlightened about shrinking so that other people won't feel insecure around you. We are born to make manifest the Glory of God that is within us; it's not just in some of us; it's in everyone. As we let our own light shine, we unconsciously give other people permission to do the same. As we are liberated from our own fear our presence automatically liberates others."

Gabriel Deeds

From, "A Return to Love," by Marianne Williamson and quoted by Nelson Mandela in his inaugural speech, 1994.

At this point I would like to introduce a very unlikely ally. This ally is more terrifying than almost anything we can conceive. Its introduction at this point might cause you to put this book down and not read another word. I am willing to risk it because this ally has an unfair reputation and can actually be hugely beneficial to our cause.

Sometimes to achieve focus, to attain that objectivity that enables us to look at ourselves frankly and honestly, we need a shock. Something so powerful that it can shatter all our little Self deceits and illusions. Something that we all share, that binds us together in the ultimate reality.

Death.

It is strange that such a natural and indisputable fact of life should be so difficult for us to accept. Many of us successfully manage to avoid reflection on the subject until the day we die. More commonly we only succeed in blotting it out until the reminders become so powerful that even our expertise in Self deceit is over matched. From the subtle first trip to the optician to the sudden loss of a dear one, life is constantly trying to remind us that time is short.

Even in our youth Grandparents die, pets are solemnly interred and children ask the awkward question,

" Where is Grandpa mum?" or as parents we rush out to buy a hamster the same colour as Freddie, the one Daddy trod on. Death is sanitised, processed and removed from our everyday life as far as possible. An undertaker whisks the body away until the funeral and then the sooner it is over the better. We shun it, giving it only the briefest of nods when we have to.

Death is like someone standing over you with a stopwatch saying,

"Stop fooling about and get on with it!" This is a positive thing and normally we would do just that. Using our intelligence and problem solving skills we would reflect, analyse, assess and implement a strategy.

For example the most stunning catastrophe brings out the bravest and the best within us. On September 11th, even as the appalling tragedy unfolded firemen, policemen and paramedics swarmed while the buildings were still collapsing. Indeed as we know many were killed they were so quick off the mark. The calamity merely stimulated the dynamic drive of our species. Why then are we seemingly unable to bring these powerful problem solving skills and dynamism to bear on the big questions.

Why are we here?
What happens to us when we die?

To some extent we have attempted to analyse, rationalise and categorise these questions. The world's religions are just that. Go to a church, mosque, synagogue, temple, follow a strict moral code and go to Heaven thereafter. These honourable religions become corrupted dogmas, and are inevitably liberally laced with complex rituals and a detailed latticework of rules and regulations, which are designed to take out much of the thinking and stress of existence. They were well named the opiate of the people. We all seek to abrogate our responsibility, to gratefully place it on the altar of a greater power and run like hell.

The problem is our innate Self awareness produces a strong need to understand our own existence. This is dangerous ground. Combine this with our successful biological strategies for survival, the Hive mentality, tribalism, competition and we have a recipe for abject misery.

That is not to say that religion cannot answer our Spiritual needs, it can. Indeed any of them can. The problem comes when we encounter problems on the Spiritual path we apply Hive mind strategies because this is what we know. Personal Salvation, Enlightenment, cannot be achieved by the Hive. It must be achieved by the individual. We each of us alone bear the responsibility of saving ourselves. The more we shirk the task the more suffering we endure until finally we reach a place where we have suffered enough and begin to look for a better way.

The Spiritual path is beyond our experience, it is a lonely way leading to new levels of awareness bereft of the comforts of the Hive. On these new plains of our existence we feel alone without support and we instinctively return to the herd. Without a strong sense of Self and courage we cannot go there.

Gabriel Deeds

We would be unwise to embark upon such a journey without a plan. Ironically we are good at planning if we only take the trouble. For some bizarre reason we simply don't bother. Why?

Personal Salvation seems intangible compared to the immediacy of our so-called real world. Many of us are not exposed to Spirituality, only the suffering that results from ignoring it. We only arrive at it when in our agony we begin to question our miserable condition. We are like salmon swimming against the current, desperately struggling against time, the elements, our enemies, the natural flow of the water. We struggle because that is what we are driven to do, what we are taught. We are not salmon, we are Human beings.

If we are to rise above mere biology we must turn and flow with the current of the Universe. We must acknowledge our Spirituality, decide what it is we believe and concentrate our efforts on the very real task of personal Salvation.

We are both the unique individual, the Spiritual mind, as well as the dutiful worker bee, the Hive mind, with its entire existence mapped out ahead of it. The one a complete anathema to the other. How then can we reconcile the two?

The Self must first flourish and grow strong within the Hive. As the Hive's influence fails and begins to diminish so the time will arise when many will begin to seek a better way

Firstly recognise the two separate parts of the whole you. One should not strive against the other. For the purposes of this book however, I will assume that the Hive mind is the dominant of the two at considerable cost to the Spiritual mind. Individual thought is dangerous to the Hive which is only concerned with successful perpetuation of the species. Following the Hive mind is by far the easier of the two routes and therefore initially the more attractive. Having taken the easier route our Spiritual mind resorts to the subconscious, the "still small voice," and merely waits an opportunity to be heard. The first heart attack or the car accident that puts you in bed for a month.

This is where Death can be an ally; it is a useful tool for destroying illusion. How does your high powered career help you in the face of Death? Where is your influence, your wealth? There is no need to fear Death, if you use your analytical, problem solving skills and your intelligence to prepare for it. It is like the half time whistle. Life is the first half in which we prepare for the second half, the afterlife. It will terrify you if you have ignored it, blocked it out. It's no good arguing with the referee when it's time and remember the big snag; we never know when our time will come. Accept Death as your friend and teacher. Even for those who do not believe in an afterlife, this life can be vastly richer and more satisfying to those who seek to understand themselves

Our ability to plan for the long term is well known. A good analogy is the pension scenario. Retirement is something that we can all contemplate, some more than others. Those who have the foresight and the discipline will enjoy a secure retirement. Those who wait until it is too late or do not bother at all, relying perhaps on the state will be in trouble. Paying your compulsory contributions which are automatically extracted from your salary is a bit like going to church for thirty years and expecting free admittance to Heaven. Fat chance.

Something more is required, you need a private plan. Even in the boring old pension stakes we display remarkable complacency and naivety, many of us ending up in poverty having to work into old age. At least we have the option of working, what happens when we die and discover that we haven't made the grade? Do you really want to find out the hard way? Are you planning to live forever?

Another good analogy is the annual holiday. It requires some work if we are going to have one. It doesn't just happen. You have to save up for it, travel agents and brochures have to be scrutinised. Deals have to be compared and negotiated, insurance, travellers cheques, cash, plastic, packing, passports getting to the airport. It's like a military operation! We don't give it a second thought, it has to be done.

We spend more time and effort in organising a single holiday than we do in preparing for our afterlives!

I am not advocating any particular religion or Spiritual practice, there are plenty of good ones to investigate. All I am saying is for your own benefit, in a purely Selfish sense, make a few enquires. Ask your Self what you believe if anything. Is this really your belief or is it something that you were brought up with? Ask a few searching questions, don't be the dope who leaves it all until it is far too late. You are the only one responsible for you, accept the job without fear of consequence. Be afraid of not acting, that is the great sin.

Reflecting on your own demise is a sure way to get you thinking. That's what this book is all about. Stop wasting all your energy on maintaining the illusion. Stop striving for material trinkets and start thinking about your next ten thousand years. Think big! You have the opportunity to evolve into a super being, an Enlightened one, or you can live like a zombie unaware, void, unfulfilled a miserable shadow. Some choice?

So let us consider your Death!

Remember that this is a positive exercise that requires courage. We all of us find things in such scrutiny that we do not like. That is the point. To move forward we need to take stock of where we are. So do not become depressed or morbid, give your Self a bit of credit, you didn't get into this mess on your own. Although you have to start out alone to repair the damage you will find help in surprising places. This book for example is simply someone else's experiences shared with you, to help.

A simple trick that I employ is to write my own epitaph. Shocking? Why? You are planning to die aren't you? I use the term lightly. Would you rather let someone else do it? For example,

> Here lies Sue Age 102
> The Good Die Young

Or

> Sacred To The Memory Of
> Captain Maurice James Butler,
> Royal Irish Rifles.
> Accidentally Shot Dead By His
> Batman On The Fourth Day Of
> April, 1882
> 'Well Done, Thou Good And Faithful Servant'

Or

Eden's Legacy

> Posterity will ne'er survey
> A nobler grave than this.
> Here lie the bones of Castlereagh
> Stop traveller and piss

(Lord Castlereagh's epitaph was said to have been written by Lord Byron. Apparently they didn't get on.)

It helps to maintain a healthy sense of humour but some are not so funny,

> My Jesus, Mercy
> Alphonse Capone
> (Mt. Carmel Cemetery; Chicago, Illinois)

Keep it short and to the point, don't ramble. Get into the spirit of the thing and have a go, it doesn't matter how good it is. What have you got to say? For example,

> Now is your time,
> Not tomorrow or yesterday,
> Today.
>
> Gabriel Deeds

It took me forty two years to write this so don't rush it, give it some thought. Write a good one and make it come true. I have noticed that most epitaphs seem to fall into two categories. Some read like an application for membership, a testimonial, and some are a message to those behind. What type will you choose?

What will they say about you when you are gone? Who will be at the graveside? Will some strange clergyman struggle to speak about someone he did not know? Will they come for the booze and the buffet? Will they come at all? Will your ashes sit unclaimed in the local crematorium to go out the back on to the rose bed when no one is looking? Is it important? You can decide how the final curtain falls, reflect upon it and begin to live your life to that end. Ignore it at your peril!

Gabriel Deeds

Now another little trick, imagine your own Death. We are on the road, it's foggy. The air is full of burning rubber and smoke, people are shouting, running. There is a tangle of metal, two cars or is it three, it's hard to tell. There is a truck at the rear half on top of the pile, all at crazy angles, welded together. There is glass and plastic all over the road. The truck driver staggers out of his cab and climbs down to the tarmac, blood is pouring from his forehead and nose. He reels towards the first car and tries to open the door. It is jammed in the mangled wreck, he puts his head through the shattered window. A man in a suit is slumped over the dash, unthinking the truck driver pulls him back into his seat, he is obviously very dead.

Recognise the corpse? Yes, it's you. There you are dead as a dodo. Too fast for you? You weren't ready? You'd like another go? Sorry, it doesn't work that way.

Here is another version. You are sipping your first coffee of the day, a small pile of mail, most of it junk lies beside you on the kitchen table. There is a plain brown envelope that looks official. You pick it up and notice that it's from the clinic. What could it be? Then you remember you had your smear test two days ago. That was fast work! You open it with the first squirming worms of anxiety stirring. They want you in right away, no explanation, no preamble, it's an instruction and that scares the hell out of you. You get on the phone first thing and there is no difficulty getting your appointment and that's scary too.

The doc lays it on the line. It's bad, it's been a while since your last smear test. You take a deep breath,

" Will you need to operate, Doctor?" He looks at you with that steady gaze and says nothing. He's done this before, his eyes tell it all. That's all folks, that's all she wrote, the end. Six weeks to six months, depending.

This life is the best chance you will ever have, stop wasting it. By anticipating Death you can plan for it. This is a dry run, an unheard of luxury that billions of those already dead would give anything for. Imagine that you are in a stadium full of ghosts, hundreds of thousands of ghosts, with you standing in the middle. You are looking bemused and undecided. They are screaming at you to get on with it, but you can't hear them. Take this opportunity seriously, or would you rather wait and negotiate with Death? (Meet Joe Black, appendix 2)

Eden's Legacy

Now find a quiet corner and write down a list of regrets. There are some sub headings below to make it easier, add your own. I'm only helping here, engage your brain. Remember, you will never speak to anyone again. You cannot go back and have another go. You are dead, imagine it, feel it. You have to participate. This book is interactive, you have work to do!

"Regret for the things we did can be tempered by time, it is regret for the things that we did not do that is inconsolable."

Sidney J. Harris

Have you told your wife that you love her recently, or the kids, or your Mum and Dad? These are just good byes, what about you and where you are going with your life. What about your afterlife? You don't know? Haven't given it much thought?

Now is a good time.

REGRETS

Family	Nearest and dearest first, then the rest.
Friends	Quality not quantity, be honest.
Partners	Something unsaid or undone?
Enemies	Former friends, partners?
Ambitions	Too much, too little, unfulfilled?
Fears	People, places, things. Has your fear held you back?
Things you have done	Ashamed, afraid, guilty?
Things you have not done	Lazy, proud, scared?
Health	Clapped out?
Beliefs	Have you got any, not sure?
Your Soul	Neglected?
Career	To busy for family? Too sneaky, dishonest, manipulative, ruthless, lazy?

Take the time do compile your list in some detail. We will need it for the Action plan in chapter 15.

<u>Please</u> **do not read any further until your list is complete.**

Eden's Legacy

You should have a lot of good material to work on at this stage. Now let's rewind, remember for the purposes of this exercise you are dead. That's right, remember the road accident? So here is a question for you. Is there anything on your list that directly relates to where you are now, i.e. dead? On your list of regrets is there anything that if done differently would have any bearing on the quality of your current afterlife? Is there anything you can point out to old St Peter that will carry any weight? Any reason why he shouldn't pull the lever on the trapdoor that you are standing on? Probably not.

In all likelihood there will be nothing on your list that indicates any kind of preparation for your afterlife. You are probably middle of the road. You would argue that you are not a bad person, whoops, that's, were, not a bad person, past tense. More to the point however, you were not a particularly good person. At this point let me apologise to the devout few who take their Spirituality, whatever form it takes, seriously. This book is aimed at the millions of us who make little or no preparation whatsoever for what they profess to believe comes after this life.

Oh you're sorry all right. Sorry about all the things you might have said and done, but what is your situation now? I don't know what you believe, you probably don't know what you believe. If at this moment, after death, you are cooking slowly over a bed of hot coals you might have one or two extra regrets to add to your list. This is an extreme example and I am not going to give you a sermon. My point is that depending on your beliefs, there is someone else on the list you may have let down. Your Self.

Ask most people and they will claim to believe in one of the popular views of what we can expect in the hereafter. Heaven or Hell, rebirth, life on another planet, it doesn't matter. Ninety percent of the population claim to believe that Death is not the end. Ask them how it effects the way they live their lives and they will shrug their shoulders.

Where are you now? Well you're dead and your asking your Self,
" Have I done enough? Will I have enough brownie points?" Get real pal. The guy with the wings and the clipboard at the front of the queue will be amazed that you even have the neck to show your face. Have you tried to understand and master your Self? What have you done to help others? Whatever you believe, you cannot avoid the dues for your

allotted four score years and ten and then expect the big bonus. Life isn't like that, neither is Death. Ask your Self honestly, do you deserve to get in?

"What, that clown, no way!"

Now review your list of regrets. Remember your beliefs. What do you truly believe will happen to you after your death? Chapter seven will help you review your beliefs. The list that you compile will reflect your beliefs. Again I include an example based on my beliefs. Don't be lazy, give it some thought, do your own list.

1. I believe in the Universal Consciousness. As a Christian, I call this power God.
2. I believe that I am a part of God and that he is a part of me.
3. I believe that I am responsible for my own Salvation and that this is my objective.
4. I believe that Self sacrifice in helping others is my route to Salvation.
5. I believe that I must live as my beliefs dictate.

This list is unique to me and to my beliefs, it dictates how I live my life and even how I think. Remember my list is not important to you, concentrate on your list. Don't waste time agreeing or disagreeing with me, do not be distracted, do your own investigation.

The same principles apply to everybody regardless of religion. If you decide that you do not believe in anything at all that's fine. All I ask is that you do your own spadework and draw your own conclusions, for your own good. You have the intelligence, you therefore have the need to understand and investigate. Make the journey and do not fear it or your Self.

"To think is to live."

Cicero.

Then, and this is important, live your life accordingly. Your life, that most precious thing, should be a conscious reflection of your beliefs, whatever they are.

Eden's Legacy

> " Diligently, seek your own Salvation."

(The dying words of Buddha)

My list of regrets is simply that I should have spent more time seeking my own Salvation.

Resources, see also appendix 1 and 2.

Books – A Return To Love.
Movies – Meet Joe Black, The Dead Poets Society,

Chapter 3   Younique

Each of us, and at this point especially you, are unique. You have heard it said many times. So many that in fact the true meaning of the word has become lost. It has been tarnished through overuse, become contemptible with easy familiarity. Our society pays lip service to the precious individual and then squashes it as an ignorant child squashes an ant. We need to re-examine this most basic truth, our uniqueness.

You are an amazing creature, yes you, now, reading this book and in your everyday life.

For now I will ignore your reaction to this statement since it does not effect the truth of it. Your reaction will probably be coloured in some way by your life experience. Interesting, but not relevant to the fact that you are a one off. There are no more of you, just one. You cannot be copied. Your perspective, your experience, your thoughts are all completely distilled and then blended into the sum of what you have been, are and will be. The essence of your Humanity contains all of this plus the secret ingredient.

Your awareness of your Self, sentience, gives you the ability to determine the objective and direction of your own life. You alone can give your life meaning. Your life is an astonishing opportunity. Realising this is ultimately the only route to Self fulfilment and peace. This is Eden's terrible Legacy, in a word, responsibility. It belongs to each individual and must be acknowledged and accepted.

We are not however, alone on this journey. The Universal Power loves us all. Do not sigh and roll your eyes, this is not some happy clappy attempt to embarrass you or entrap you. Ninety percent of us claim to believe in Life after Death. We claim to believe in a God, the label you use matters not at all.

The Universal Power will cherish and nurture each one of us that takes the first tiny step towards accepting this responsibility and living our lives accordingly. Whatever the task, no matter how terrible it may seem, the Universal Power will be with you. It will delight in the challenge and, if you are true, it will give you whatever resources, Spiritual, mental and even material, that you require. Although do not be surprised if what you get is not exactly what you ask for! Sometimes the answer is no. Sometimes we confuse our needs with our wants.

There is also a world community of individuals on the same journey. Not just in the present but in the past. Fellow travellers on the Path have stored up their wisdom in the written word. Their hard won knowledge is there for all who would seek it out.

Much comfort and strength may be gathered from our living fellow travellers, seek them out. Feelings of loneliness and isolation are common on the Path. You will be amazed at how many there are. There are also many millions who with a little encouragement would join the Quest.

To tap into this limitless store of energy and love each traveller must understand the nature of the task and the weight of the responsibility that it brings. They must then take up their burden willingly and accept it as their life's work. Each one of us must diligently seek our own Salvation.

Accepting responsibility for our own Salvation transforms us into truly powerful people. In the Spiritual sense you will become a Super-Being on the True Path. Thereafter all that matters is that you stay on it. There is no hierarchy there are only those on the Path and those who have yet to find it.

This must be the bedrock of your existence. From this foundation you can confidently build as your conscience dictates, without restriction or limits. You can spend your life quietly gardening or become the Leader of a new Faith. These things are not measured in terms of status or power or wealth. They are a matter for each individual and determined through diligent reflection and examination of the Truth. If each of us concentrated primarily on our own Salvation our world would be transformed.

This is not an easy Path to take. To walk this way will mean great sacrifice and pain. The difference will be in knowing that you suffer for a purpose rather than in darkness and ignorance. Life is full of suffering, let it be for a reason.

There is a catch in all of this. Should you achieve understanding and perceive your responsibility as I have described it then the Holy Grail, the cup of Christ, full to the brim is freely offered. You must drink from it.

To turn back to your old existence is impossible. The knowledge cannot be unlearned, it will haunt you and increase your suffering turning your life into a dreadful torment. Sooner or later in your agony you will return to drink. Again the Golden Chalice will be freely offered and one day you will drink.

Buddhists believe that this is the cycle of illusion, the Wheel of Life upon which we struggle in a seemingly aimless fashion. They believe it can take many lifetimes to even achieve Human birth. To be born Human with all the potential that this implies is incredibly auspicious. Such a precious opportunity must not be squandered.

Here you are then, that most rare creature. Not just a Human but since you are reading this book, a sentient individual. Not because of this book, but because you are actively searching. You are poised upon the threshold of creations greatest adventure. This is a very great responsibility. To proceed requires great courage, strength and wisdom.

Terrifying things will be required of you. Each of us fears different things. It could be something dramatic like a change of career, new friends, even new family. Who can say where the Path will lead?

The next step is literally that. You must consciously step onto the Path. That single step will separate you from the greater mass of creation writhing in the darkness of ignorance, fear, and intolerance.

Remember that in a strictly Selfish sense you are doing all this for your own Salvation. Focus on this point, it is beautifully simple, this is all for you. This is the core of your life's work. In time you will realise that you are truly a precious commodity, believe it, it is true. It is alright to think this way even if you feel guilty doing it.

How can it be right to be so selfish? In time you will realise that your own Salvation is completely dependent on that of your fellow beings. For now it is vital that the foundation is laid for all your future efforts. That foundation is you, precariously but firmly on the Path.

You can do nothing until you have begun to seek your own Salvation. Then and only then can you begin to help others. To wade straight into good works no matter how laudable without knowledge of Self is merely Self deceit.

Very few things in life are black and white. Rather there are endless variations on a theme. So it is with our consciousness. It is like being on a spiral staircase. No matter where we are on the staircase we can look up or down. We can see where we have been and looking up we can see where we are going.

As we climb we meet others, some going up some going down. We are not higher or lower we are just at a different place. Occasionally we come to a place we recognise. Here we realise that we have through Self deceit or weakness, gone astray. When we realise we stop and patiently begin to climb again.

There are always people ahead and behind, sometimes if we are fortunate they travel with us for a time. Teachers, friends or just companions. These can help us on our journey.

We may meet a traveller seemingly going in the wrong direction, coming down the staircase. Remember that your position on the staircase is not a measure of success or failure. It is relative to your own unique journey and cannot be compared to that of another.

Someone coming down may have been where you hope to be and know more than you. Someone passing you on the steps going up may know the way having been there already. You may meet them later going the other way.

It matters only that you are on the Path, consumed by your individual struggle for Enlightenment.

As we struggle forward we must have compassion for ourselves. We will make mistakes and stray sometimes so far from the way that we feel we can never recover. No matter how far we stray, no matter how bad we think we are the Universal Power will wait for us to catch up. If our intentions are pure it will help and guide us. We are so loved.

In this seemingly selfish mode of existence you will become intimate with pain and suffering. You will gradually begin to perceive others also suffering in a new light.

"Yes Brother, I fell there at that same obstacle many times." Or,

"Yes Sister it was many years before I understood as you now understand."

As we watch others struggle, we gradually realise that they are not competitors, but fellow sufferers. As we see them struggle we are overcome with the desire to help. In the same moment and in future acts of compassion so we step onto a new level on the staircase.

So it is through the selfish pursuit of our own Salvation comes the realisation that our destinies are intertwined inextricably with those of our fellow human beings. We take a quantum leap in our own journey when we realise that we cannot win alone. We cannot even cross the finish line until we have gone back to help those struggling behind. **How could you attain peace or Enlightenment knowing that others still suffer? It cannot be. If they suffer, you suffer.**

We must try to change our Society's way of thinking, to see things as they really are. The biological process of evolution, survival of the fittest, must be superseded by the struggle for Enlightenment. Ironically this is in itself an evolutionary strategy, the only one that will succeed.

Resources, see also appendix 1 and 2.

Books – Ethics For The New Millennia.
Movies- Ghandi

Eden's Legacy

Chapter 4   Born into conflict

From the day of your birth to the day of your death your life will be full of conflict. Conflict is the cauldron into which we are plunged with our first breath as the midwife slaps us on the arse.

As a unique individual you will have your own perspective and ways. The world is full of other individuals with their separate needs and wants and naturally there will be a clash. The seemingly stifling constraints that our peers and society place on us as individuals have evolved to control internal conflict so that we may dominate other species.

The individual is restrained by the Tribe for the common good. Over millennia this successful strategy has become ingrained to such an extent that all non-human opposition has been eliminated. The individual is now not merely restrained but oppressed.

By our very nature we are destined to compete and strive so that only the strongest will prosper. The Self is driven underground, carefully camouflaged, eventually denied. In this arena it seems that the only way to attain Self goals is to learn to manipulate and exploit others. The very objective and goals we choose to set for ourselves are corrupted by the desire to be accepted and to win.

On an individual level this is very destructive but since the individual is the basic building block then whole societies adopt the same approach. The result is a huge vicious circle of intolerance, aggression, and competition for resources.

As we use up our planet and it's resources so then the conflict grows. Ultimately it will be the tool by which our species is culled to sustainable levels to begin the cycle again. However with our technological capabilities we are the first species to have the capacity to destroy, not only ourselves, but the whole planet.

This is inevitable given time, unless we begin the process of understanding and modifying our behaviour. This will take many generations and must begin with the education of our children.

Somehow, through the use of our own intelligence, we must instil new values into our young. Traditional Spiritual beliefs must become successful evolutionary strategies if we are to avoid catastrophe. If we fail, then Mother Nature will step in. She is a cold and ruthless master.

It may be that realisation can only dawn after calamity has decimated the human population. If we are fortunate we may get another chance, after a very hard lesson. Better by far, surely, if we could begin now.

Children learn about conflict from an early age. They learn that they cannot always have what they want. They learn the arts of negotiation, manipulation and compromise quickly. However there is an old saying,

"Youth and enthusiasm will always be defeated by experience and cunning."

In short the child is at a disadvantage from the start. Parents are much more adept at competing in the rat race. Fortunately they are also strongly disposed to give their children what they want. So there is a kind of balance between what the child wants and what the parents feel that she should have.

As a parent this balance should be one of our most important daily considerations. Indeed it should be considered before even thinking of having children. In fact it is often not considered at all. What the child receives is a random mish-mash of tradition, what is acceptable and what the parent is prepared to give.

It is a sad fact that most parents give little or no objective thought as to how their children should be nurtured. All too often children just happen. Having children is expected and they become product in the vast machine we have constructed to "take care" of our children. The child then competes for our attention and love.

We in turn become so embroiled in the struggle to bring up our families that we spend our lives fighting to survive and prosper. No different from wild animals we exist in a biological sense and compete against each other for more of everything. The child becomes inured to competition, that seemingly necessary evil. It is a life skill that we pick up and hone like a sharp blade.

We are controlled by other people and their expectations until we can overthrow and control them. How is the child controlled? Through a systematic and cumulative attack on the child's Self confidence. (See chapter 5) Another person's success is a threat, their failure, cause for celebration. Whatever thinking we do falls into the category of scheming and plotting. We are consumed by the struggle and distracted from the truth. We create for ourselves an unhappy, destructive, illusory world in which we writhe and twist until we can no longer endure it. At this point we have no idea what to do so we return to what we know.

We teach our children to fight as we have fought. We teach that life is full of suffering and hardship. Unconsciously we pass on our twisted beliefs and bad habits without thought or reflection. Our lives are full of pain and conflict, much of it futile, serving only to perpetuate the species and thus the cycle of suffering.

It is no longer enough to be the strongest, we must become the wisest, most educated and Spiritual of species. It is no longer enough for a few individuals to see the light. Our species must collectively change its ways or be doomed to become extinct on a barren rock or be devastated by war, famine and disease.

If we are ever to take our place in the stars we must retain our biological vigour and temper it with Self knowledge. We must open our minds and display a willingness to move on Spiritually and mentally. We have the knowledge and experience scattered within existing cultures and within the pages of history and literature. We must somehow unite the Human race in distilling and refining all of this in a common objective, in the final conflict.

As a combative species we do best when we have a common enemy to unite us. If we could invent a race of aliens bent on colonising earth, Human kind would rise up as one and fight. Give us an obvious enemy and we will eventually prevail. The real enemies, ignorance, intolerance fear and greed are not so easy to defeat. They are insidious, elusive, they are a part of us. That race of Evil aliens is already here, it's us. If we had the technology and the opportunity we would find some excuse to colonise every planet in the galaxy.

The mastery of Self is our only hope. From our inability to govern ourselves comes all the suffering to which we are chained in endless conflict. The individual Self is the basic building block of our society. From Presidents to toddlers we are all individuals who will ultimately stamp their mark on society.

The individual, you, is the battlefield upon which the forces of Good and Evil ceaselessly struggle to place their flags. You are the greatest prize of all. Neither side can win until you decide to take your place in the conflict. You alone have the power to determine the outcome.

This is Eden's Legacy, you alone have inherited the power to seal your own fate.

The powers of Evil, through the Hive, blind you to this truth and makes you fearful of the terrible responsibility that must come with this inheritance. It does not have to defeat Good to win it merely has to stop you from taking part. It hides your birthright in deceit and illusion. It whispers in your ear,
"Better the Devil you know".
In the agony thus created, in this artificial environment of endless pain, ignorance, bigotry and greed lounge like princes in a palace. The palace we have created for ourselves and for them. Hell on earth. The minute we realise our legacy and take up our burden they are evicted, cast out. You hold that power. If you only knew just how important you really are.

Resources, see also appendix 1 and 2.

Books - Lord of the Rings.
Movies – A Man For All Seasons.

Chapter 5   Self confidence

Self confidence is the freedom to express your true nature. It is a belief in your Self, and an understanding of your true value. With Self confidence you have the ability to deal with any situation. It is the deciding factor in the eternal struggle between Good and Evil.

In the age old struggle for your Soul how much Self confidence you have determines whether or not you will fly with God or wither here on a hellish earth. Even God's happiness is dependant on your victory. He cannot be content until you come home, the Universe is waiting for you. I can't put it any stronger than that.

How could you be more important?

Even for the non Spiritual your Self confidence determines how happy you are going to be now and in the future. If you have it, anything is possible, without it, you will never reach your full potential. To be truly Self confident you must recognise and study your Self and be aware of the threats and opportunities you will face. For most of us this means learning through bitter experience.

As with all things related to Self no two people are the same. It is a question of degree and relativity, however, the underlying processes are the same. My examples are only to clarify the process, please don't be distracted by what happened to me. Concentrate on your Self and what happened to you.

Self confidence has a cycle of its own which must be understood. As babies we are given it with our Mother's milk. As children and in our youth it is stolen from us, and as adults we must recover it. Once lost it cannot be returned, even by God. It has to be rediscovered, we must claw it back in the painful process that is referred to in many religious texts as rebirth. As we are reborn so we must learn to love ourselves as our Mother's loved us. We must reconstruct ourselves in the light of our growing awareness and Enlightenment. This is easier to do if we understand why Self confidence was taken from us in the first place and how it was done.

So why is Self confidence taken from us? Self confidence is power but power alone is not enough. If we are allowed to possess it without the benefit of wisdom derived from suffering we are like a callow youth who thinks he knows everything and yet knows nothing. We are misled by our own arrogance and so ultimately fail to begin the process of Enlightenment. It is inevitable that we will suffer until we can learn from suffering. The Hive takes our Self confidence so that we can be controlled and dominated. It seeks to hide the power and value of Self from us. The Universal Power allows it to be taken from us because as sentient beings we must each make our own choices. The Universal Power cannot take away our responsibility no matter how much we want it to.

Reborn Self confidence, if achieved, is tempered by our experience and suffering. It is purged of arrogance in the fire of our pain and humiliation. Its edge is finely honed by the power of our compassion for those who suffer as we have suffered. As we are immersed in the process of rebirth the powers of Good and Evil struggle to influence us. The one for our glorious Enlightenment the other for our perpetual enslavement. The battle is fought within you, your life is the gory battle ground, a stricken field.

In the age old conflict of Good verses Evil you hold the balance of power. In some ways more powerful than either Good or Evil since you have what both sides want, you're Self. We are terrified of this responsibility and want only to sit on the fence. Most of us seek to avoid the choice but in so doing we actually make the wrong decision.

You and you alone, have the power to free your Self, you must consciously choose which path to take.

It is you who must take the white hot blade of your Self from the very fires of Hell with your bare hands and plunge it into the cool depths of the Universe's love for you. Until you realise this and act you are doomed to repeat an endless cycle of suffering.

Our Self confidence once rediscovered is purified and strengthened. This is the only way that we can acquire true wisdom, humility and compassion. If we fail to accept the challenge of our own responsibility we are doomed to endure enslavement and suffering without purpose. Such a living hell can only be endured until we have learned the Truth of Self and developed the confidence to accept its responsibilities. How much can you endure before realisation dawns?

That is the why. The how Self confidence is taken from us is the saddest tale you will ever hear. As I speak children all over the world are being abused in a thousand different ways and the Angels weep tears of grief and frustration unable to intervene. Ah yes, we like to blame God for what we do, but we are responsible, not God. Evil flourishes in our hearts until we learn to understand and control Self.

The sooner the Hive attacks the child the easier it is to strip away Self confidence. We see this in the dead, killer's eyes of the six year old child soldier. He is forced to kill a relative before he is allowed to live and to pick up the rifle that is bigger than he is. Such inconceivable violence is common in our world. It is not inconceivable at all, is it? We see it every night on the television.

Babies are raped because some ignorant savages believe that Aids can be cured by having sex with a virgin. How else can you find a virgin these days? A tourist is stabbed and robbed so the police pour petrol into the sewers and set it on fire to drive out the half human children who call the sewer home. In China where a second child is prohibited and everyone wants a boy, girls are regularly abandoned on the rubbish dump.

Most children in the West are born into a nurturing environment. We might think we don't have to worry, our children have loving parents to protect them. Not so. The dangers are less dramatic but they are powerful, insidious and incredibly violent none the less. The Hive will always find a way to attack the child, always. What weapons does it use? How can children in the prosperous West be attacked and stripped of their Self esteem and Self confidence?

The most potent weapons for the stripping of Self confidence are the parent and the teacher.

Initially everything is well ordered and the child's status assured. They are fed and clothed and, I pray, loved. Self confidence comes easily. It is as natural for a child as breathing. Fear is almost unknown. The two however, Self confidence and fear, are inextricably linked. As one waxes the other wanes. The proportion of the mix is critical. Quite simply, it determines how much suffering and unhappiness we endure, or, put another way, how much joy and happiness we acquire.

One of our earliest and most powerful fears is that of abandonment. Will Mum be there to look after me and comfort me? Here, right at the very start of our existence the pattern is set. How much happiness or suffering we encounter, even our survival, depends on someone else. It depends on our interaction with another person or people.

This ongoing relationship with our fellow human beings is absolutely pivotal to the balance of our existence! Sentience, Spiritual Salvation is a far distant horizon we may or may not reach.

The power of human interaction is absolutely shocking in its potency.

It completely eclipses any other power for a child and indeed for most adults. Even love at this early stage is unknown except through interaction with others.

We are addicted to our relationships, convinced that alone we must be miserable and unhappy. We seek the romantic illusion of a soul mate, convinced that without a mate we cannot be whole. We try to make up for our own inadequacies by attaching ourselves to someone else. Friends, partners, leaders almost anyone will do. The concept of Self is terrifying, small wonder considering the way in which we are brought up.

This is a fatal flaw, this dependence on others and avoidance of Self would suffice for baboons but not for sentient humanity. For us it leads only to torment and illusion. We are distracted from our own Self worth and from Self fulfilment. We all begin life as do baboons. Survival, conflict and inter personal relationships dominate our lives and we are brainwashed by our early experiences. As our sentience exerts itself we begin to question and the true nature of humanity struggles out of the baboon like a butterfly emerging from the grub.

The longer we put off this process the more pain we endure until it becomes unendurable. Recognise the inevitability of your ultimate emergence right now, cut to the chase. After all we are supposed to be intelligent.

Until then however, how much Self confidence we have depends largely on how this interaction with others occurs. This is a major problem especially for children who are so dependent on the adults around them. Sooner or later the child's needs clash with those of the other individuals around it and the conflict begins.

Consider your own Self confidence within the privacy of your own thoughts. Nobody is listening, you can be honest with your Self if you try. Recall your Self as a small child still unaffected by the attack on your Self confidence. The smiling, confident child that was you. Remember that child. Remember a time, from your earliest memories and go through the photo albums. Find a picture of your Self as that carefree child, one that you like. Have it framed and put it somewhere you can see it every day. I keep mine beside my monitor. Remind your Self of what you were, what you still are, precious, loveable, loved. Go find that photograph, right now.

By reconstructing the crimes that were committed against you can understand,

1. The incredible violence done to you and to your oppressors.
2. Your own natural vulnerability and innocence.
3. The power you hold and your responsibility to break the cycle of suffering.

The chief tools in the destruction of Self confidence are,

1. Humiliation
2. Negative Criticism
3. Fear

These bloody instruments of torture and especially our fear of them are used indiscriminately on each of us throughout our lives. It is not the power of each individual experience but the frequency and relentless nature of the attack. Sometimes the fear of the lash does more damage than the lash itself. The damage is cumulative, this is a war of attrition. Hence the wry old adage,

"Don't let the bastards grind you down."

They do though, don't they?

Take the photograph of your Self in your hand and consider the most humiliating events in your life. Consider the criticism you have endured, where did it come from. Begin as far back as you can, count the scars one by one slowly and carefully. Focus your thoughts on the people who mattered and perhaps still do and then against activities in which you have been humiliated or criticised. Consider how these experiences and the feelings thus evoked have affected your personality. If you could go through it again how would you change things?

There will be dramatic, painful examples that you can instantly recall but don't overlook the long term low grade examples. My Father never once said to me,

"Well done." The absence of something can be just as wearing as a bad experience. I recognise now that giving praise was not in his make up. He was trained in a brutal school and suffered terribly all his life from low Self esteem and a lack of Self confidence.

His life did indeed set me an example. It took me forty years to work out the lesson contained in his life and how it interacted with my family and with me. It is a bitter thing to see a life wasted, a horrible realisation. As the Hive measure things he was successful. He was an educated professional man of means. Big house plenty of money, but in every important way his life was a desert. He died of Alzheimers, to all intents and purposes he starved to death after years in a nursing home. His body could no longer absorb nourishment, he was unconscious, unaware. He died as he lived.

Was my Father's life wasted? By him, debatable, but it certainly will not be wasted by me. The lesson was well learned, eventually, I learned it! There is a lesson here for all of us.

Life's suffering must teach us or it is futile.

My Father was never able to understand and repair the damage done to him. He never really had a chance. By learning and becoming aware we can overcome any injury and turn defeat into victory, darkness into light. Yes it requires courage, integrity and compassion to give your life, you're suffering, meaning, but look at the alternative. Perhaps my father's life was a success, perhaps his seemingly shocking life and death will help trigger the light of realisation in others through me. I will struggle to make it so. In so doing I have already won. I can be beaten, but never defeated.

As you compile your list of those who have undermined your Self confidence, humiliated and criticised you, there is one name you cannot overlook. Your own. Another horrible side effect of this war of attrition is the way in which it recruits the victim. Eventually you start to believe the criticism, the humiliation eats away at your Self confidence until you become your own worst critic.

Once again I say, you hold the ultimate power. Nobody, but nobody, can do more damage to your Self than you. Not only to you, but to the people around you, even your own children. Nobody but you has the power and the responsibility to save your Self. Any feelings of low esteem and Self confidence are merely illusions generated to neutralise your innate power. The Hive corrupts your own energy and turns it against you. The Hive does not care whether or not you hold any Spiritual beliefs. You are merely cannon fodder, grist to the mill. It is unfeeling, insensible, its influence however is powerful. Good or Evil comes only from us depending on how we are influenced and how aware we are.

The simple truth is that it is up to you to make a conscious choice.

The table on page 53 might help to structure things, but first here are some of my examples to start you off.

I was in my mid twenties before I began to realise that I wasn't stupid. I was born in East Africa and travelled extensively as a child from country to country. My first language was Swahili, I was a late starter in reading and writing English. I was always arriving at a new school with the wrong accent and a different curriculum. I am also an inveterate day dreamer. Teachers just adored me.

There have been countless times when I was hauled up to the front of the class and humiliated. I remember them all. I mention some of them now not to evoke pity but to demonstrate the potency of these acts of brutality. Remember that they were perpetrated on a child by teachers.

At the age of about seven I was almost illiterate. I arrived at an Australian State school and made the acquaintance of Miss Fisher. I was a major fly in the ointment of her well ordered life. I could not answer

Gabriel Deeds

her questions and took refuge in my day dreams. She would rush through the other children, seize me by the wrist and haul me dramatically out of the class, through the playground and into the infants class where I had to stand in the corner while the little ones looked on wide eyed. She did this most days.

When I was twelve I started the new term and joined my old class, N2B, and the kids with whom I had spent the previous term. About twenty minutes into the lesson a prefect knocked on the door called out my name and announced that I was in the wrong class. I had been demoted to N2C, the "duffers" class. I remember getting my stuff together in the silent classroom, I remember that long walk to the door.

I was quite a small, slight child and I remember one biology class in which we were talking about natural selection. I was sitting next to Mills, a hulking prefect in the elite first fifteen rugby squad. Dr Hickey made the two of us stand up side by side. Throughout the lesson he referred to Mills as a magnificent specimen compared to me the "poor waif." Everybody laughed at my expense, including me. How horrible that a child should laugh at his own torture, how horrible that this was done by a teacher in the classroom. It is true that we always remember our teachers.

My school was prestigious and expensive. It had its own swimming pool. I can remember my first experience of it clearly. I was in a large class with one teacher. Mr Robins was a dapper little martinet, very scary. It was very simple. We were told to jump in and swim round and around the pool while he read his newspaper. As you would expect there were all shapes and sizes and degrees of expertise within the class.

I choked and spluttered my way around the pool until half drowned I vomited. I was vilified and humiliated by all and sundry. The other kids thought it was a hoot and Mr Robins was mad. Of course the simple truth was that I couldn't swim.

I could recount dozens of these stories. The sad thing is that the damage done was compounded by the fact that my Father went to just such a school and suffered a similar fate. He was always critical, not just with me but with everyone. It is the same with most bullies. They are damaged goods. If you are bullied you become a bully. If you are abused you abuse, it doesn't matter how. There are always bullies, every child is afflicted by them.

Eden's Legacy

Aitken was an especially bad example. He was tall and lean and completely psychotic. On one terrible occasion I was chatting away to someone over my shoulder when to my horror I walked straight into Aitken. In front of everyone he snarled down at me ripping the bag of crisps I had been eating out of my hands. He rolled them up into a ball and flung them into my face. I can still remember his expression. He stepped back and kicked me right in the testicles.

As I fell to the ground I remember seeing my friends studiously looking the other way. I imagined they were embarrassed and ashamed of me and my weakness, just as I was. In actual fact they were probably just glad it wasn't them. It simply would not occur to them to intervene, just as it never occurred to me when I saw others abused. The bully injures everybody involved not just the victim but the onlookers, himself and especially the adults who permit this behaviour. Their culpability is inescapable.

These are common examples of what can happen to children. Corrosive, cumulative, systematic, humiliation. As a child I felt somehow that I should have been better than I was. I was always embarrassed, humiliated, attacked. I came to expect it of people in general. I was not aware of the deficiencies of others only my own perceived deficiencies. I was not at fault merely, different.

I became a human tortoise so that when a frustrated teacher hauled me up to answer a deliberately easy question I didn't even hear the words. Deep in my shell I sheltered from attack and so the teacher became more frustrated and the other children saw me as stupid. Their opinion of me became my opinion of my Self. All because I had lost the confidence to answer a simple question. Over the decades, that's how long it takes, I became aware of what had happened to me and my own innocence and vulnerability.

The only way to repair such damage is to understand the process. Remember your own experiences will be different, it is the process that is important. Tease out every injury, examine the perpetrator and the victim. Examine your feelings and the effects these experiences have had on you. How have they affected your personality?

You must become aware of this cycle and its effects on you. Above all be particularly watchful for a tendency to treat others as you have been treated.

Gabriel Deeds

If you become that which you loathed and feared as a child, then truly you are not just injured, but crippled.

Not irredeemably, for none are so far from hope, but the price for ignoring the example and lesson of your own suffering is a heavy one.

There must be no room in your life for bitterness, revenge or recrimination. The cycle must be broken, this can only be done through a raising of your awareness. You must also be aware of the damage the perpetrators of these actions have suffered themselves. They too are victims, be compassionate towards your Self and to them. They may still be trapped in this eddy in the cycle of suffering. You have the opportunity to step outside this miserable destructive cycle and move on.

Your Self confidence can be rebuilt from your awareness and understanding. As you are attacked in future it may be that because you can see past the attack itself, understanding the causes and the effects, you can neutralise the venom and break the cycle, turning the other cheek as it were. Not passively but from a position of Enlightened awareness.

Do not underestimate the damage done and do not hesitate to utilise whatever resources you can to combat the effects and understand your Self. Professional help from a councillor or a psychiatrist is often very rewarding and can dramatically accelerate a process that you might never complete alone. It is also good to recognise and acknowledge your scars and your own limited ability to deal with them. You don't have to do this alone. As a sentient being in a civilised society there is no shame in seeking help. It is an Enlightened, intelligent thing to do.

Help is available all over the place. Before you can utilise it however, you must recognise your Self as a reformed victim. No longer will you put up with being treated like this. You now see the Hive and what it has done. You are aware. You now have the Self respect which frees you to begin to recover your Self confidence.

Below is a check list to help you identify those powerful damaging experiences and the more low key long term forms of damaging behaviour that sap Self confidence. Remember, this is purely about you, there are no comparisons in this exercise. What affects you and how, is unique to you and therefore important.

Eden's Legacy

Somebody raised in the projects of New York would laugh at my experiences. A child brought up in the streets of Freetown might think me fortunate to be educated and brought up in the West. We all have our crosses to bear, all are equally valid and important.

Gabriel Deeds

Self Confidence

*mild to ***** extreme

Source	Humiliation	Criticism	Failure
Father		****	****
Mother			
Siblings			
Relatives			
Friends			
Enemies	****		
Teachers	*****	****	****
Partners	**		
Bosses	***	***	
Colleagues	***		
Strangers	**		***
Activities			
Academic	****	**	****
Work	***	**	
Sex	**		
Appearance	***	**	

Eden's Legacy

Even a quick trip down this gauntlet of memory lane will provide you with ample proof of the things that have been done to you. Even the most confident amongst us carry the deep wounds that erode our Self confidence and drive the secret being within each of us further and further underground. Indeed the outward signs of confidence are often merely part of the projected self that we use to ward off attack. When it comes to Self confidence things are seldom as they seem.

You should see your Self as the victim in this exercise, however most of us feel to blame in some way. Recognise that you are also trained to attack. You contain both elements within you, victim and assailant. You must work on understanding and controlling both aspects of your Self. The cycle of suffering can only be broken when you accept what was done to you and what you have done to others.

This is the Hive's greatest strength. All of its victims become its advocates and so the cycle is perpetuated. Every teacher that humiliated us was humiliated, every bully was bullied. Our parents often repeat the errors that their parents made. If you have children be vigilant against reflecting your own injuries in their lives. As a young man those close to me could always stop me in my tracks with the simple retort,

"You're just like your Father."

Nobody knows you as well as you know your Self. Consider your personality. What traits would you like to eliminate or highlight. I am particularly vulnerable in social situations. I find it very difficult to trust people since I am constantly expecting to have to defend myself from attack. This often manifests itself as aggression towards people I regard as a threat. I find it very difficult to commit to relationships for the same reason. I am excessively independent, almost reclusive. I am a reluctant misanthrope. I would like to be a social animal but for me it is very difficult to overcome my experience of humiliation at the hands of the bullies in my life. For me people are like fire, I like to warm my hands but I never get too close.

As you go through this exercise recognise the outward forces that have acted against you over the years. Recognise your vulnerability and the violence that has been done to you. Forget blame, revenge and bitterness, these are the tools with which the Hive turns you from innocent victim to willing accomplice. What matters is that you understand the conflict that is taking place and recognise the part that

Gabriel Deeds

you must play. Your pain and suffering will make you wise and create within you the compassion for others that will be the driving force of your future existence.

Resources, see also appendix 1 and 2.

Books – The Power Of One, How To Develop Self confidence, (Carnegie.)
Movies – Barney The Dinosaur, (rediscover the innocence of a child) Bugs life, Tom Brown's Schooldays.

Section Two

Chapter 6-8   Personal Audit, where am I?

Chapter Six: The secret being

1. Suppression
2. Is anybody there?
3. A solid foundation

Chapter Seven: What do you believe?

1. Upbringing
2. Experience
3. Conclusion

Chapter Eight: Success, a new definition

1. Pecking order
2. Self deceit
3. Peace

Chapter 6   The Secret Being

We are all of us connected to the central consciousness of the Universe. We sprang from it and ultimately will return to it. Very few of us truly believe that there is nothing except today and perhaps tomorrow followed by nothing. We squabble and argue about doctrinal details even going to war in the name of our particular religion. Seldom do we recognise the role that we have to play as individuals.

The Secret Being within each of us is suppressed, hushed like a child likely to cause embarrassment. It is much easier to accept the role of the drone, to do what is expected and therefore to be accepted. To acknowledge the inner Self means accepting responsibility for our own destiny and being prepared, if necessary to stand up and say,

" No! This is wrong."

It means recognising that each of us must realise our own importance and accept that how we act is important, vital. It is too easy to say,

"What can I do? What can one person do?"

This is a lazy, weak attitude, the result of low Self esteem which allows the Hive to prosper within us. When we feel ineffectual we are ineffectual, impotent. When we turn away from our responsibilities we allow Evil to prosper and condemn ourselves to Self loathing and suffering. Why do we do this? We are better than that.

Being Good is not in defeating Evil, it is in fighting it without thought of victory or cost simply because you know that it is wrong.

If we do not fight because we feel we cannot win or because we feel that the cost is too high then indeed we have failed. We might see it as biding our time or even feel that we can sit on the fence and at least save ourselves. The truth is in so doing we have enslaved ourselves to futile suffering and handed victory to the Dark side.

We know this to be true and yet, somehow it always applies to someone else, not us personally. The principle of standing up to the bully is well known to us. Who among us has not been bullied or more

Eden's Legacy

importantly had our behaviour modified by the actions of a bully on someone else? It is an excellent metaphor for our lives and may help you to understand your own predicament. The Hive is primarily a bully.

The bully is only a problem when he can divide and isolate the individual Self. Even that is not enough, he can only succeed if he can brow beat the chosen individual into inaction. This inaction is what he is after, it is his lifeblood. First he paralyses the individual and then through fear, sucks him dry.

The bully is like the lion looking for a gazelle. He chooses his victim carefully. The small, quiet kid, the one who does not have allies who might defend him. The tactic is simple, by viciously attacking his prey openly he sends a message to the rest of the group.

" Don't cross me or you might get the same treatment."

In so doing he commits an act of unspeakable violence. What is the nature of this violence? This Evil act is aimed at the Self esteem of the individual where it is perhaps most destructive in one sense. Worse it attacks the Self esteem of every person who does not act. You may confidently assert that you have never been bullied. You couldn't be more wrong. If one of us is bullied, we are all bullied.

Everyone who fails to act is condemned to be dominated by the bully, suffering enough you might think. Much worse is the humiliation and Self loathing we endure when we allow ourselves to be controlled through our own cowardice.

Soon the bully has accomplices, hangers on who add to the menace and influence of the bully. We know all about it, it's an old story,

"Seig Heil."

The suffering we choose to endure in this way is much, much worse than we would endure in fighting back. Even if the bully beats us up and seems to win, in fact he is defeated. (The Mission, appendix 2). As long as we fight him he cannot win, I do not mean with mere violence. Violence begets violence and those who use it are ensnared by the Hive. We must stand up for ourselves when he attacks us and especially when he attacks someone else in front of us.

So why is it that we are cursed by our own inaction?

Gabriel Deeds

The suppression of Self begins early. It is insidious and relentless at an age when we can scarcely be expected to know what it is that is attacking us, let alone defend ourselves. So when does it start? We all know when, when did you meet your first bully? You may as well say when was your first memory.

For most of us bullying is something that we learn about at school. (School again!) It may as well be on the curriculum. By the time we are a little older our Secret Being is so heavily scarred that we have hidden it deep, it is so camouflaged we can barely find it ourselves. We are inured to the chains of the bullying Hive, inaction is our middle name.

Our Self confidence has been eroded and we learn to be cautious about intervening or standing up for ourselves or for others. We have eaten so much crow pie, humiliation, that we don't feel we can influence events. We cry,

"What can I do?" What we should be saying is,

"What should I do?"

The extent of this suppression, this inaction is devastating, it can scarcely be believed.

In a psychological study fourteen actors and one member of the public were placed in a lecture room to fill out forms. The actors were told to ignore everything and continue to fill out the forms. A few minutes later smoke started to come under the doors. Everybody except the one member of the public knew it was fake. The scientists watched as the lone individual anxiously watched the smoke. He immediately turned to the other members of the class to see their reaction. He asked out loud,

"Is that smoke?" He was ignored. His fellow students were unmoved by the smoke and continued to fill out their forms. Although obviously anxious he took his lead from the group and returned to his forms.

In a televised orienteering team event three teams set off at the same time. One team pulled ahead slightly and turned in completely the wrong direction. The other teams followed in the wrong direction. How does this happen? It is easier and more comfortable to follow the herd even if it is wrong. The lone individual is soon destroyed, the group is our best chance. This is how we have been conditioned and where our instincts take us. It is hard to take responsibility and perhaps make a mistake. Especially when you don't think much of your Self.

So there is group behaviour based on survival and then there is the behaviour of individuals within the group. There is always a pecking order and that means competition, conflict, survival of the fittest. No matter where you are in the pecking order there is always someone above you and below you. The result is constant turmoil. This is fine for baboons but hardly a fitting template for life as sentient human beings! Yet it is the one that we commonly adhere to.

This system is designed by Mother Nature for biological procreation, the Hive. The moment we become sentient, Self aware and responsible for our individual and collective consciousness this system becomes redundant. Alas we have been unable to collectively replace this system with another, largely because we are not born sentient. We may become sentient. Some come to it early some late, some not at all. It's an individual thing and the Hive does not like individuals.

Most sentients are realised in middle age by which time terrible damage has been wrought by the Hive. Further development is therefore much more difficult if not impossible. Imagine if we taught our children about their Spiritual birthright and encouraged them to take responsibility for themselves and each other. Some day perhaps we will, or perhaps our sentience can only be born through suffering? True no doubt, but only to a certain extent. Suffering should come to teach us on the Way not as a result of avoiding it. Our children need our help to begin their own journey.

At school we had a canteen. At lunchtime we would all line up and wait to be filed in to sit at the tables. At each table there were two prefects, one at each end to supervise the meal. Most of the prefects were fair some were not. Concord, so named because of his nose, was not fair.

At his table everybody's portion was carefully halved. We received one half and the two prefects the other. There were eight at a table including the prefects so there were six victims. Both prefects in total ate two and a half meals, whilst we had half a meal. Nobody ever complained to the teachers who were sitting nearby. Inaction.

Gabriel Deeds

Concord was well known and as we queued at the door we tried to make sure we were so placed in the queue that we would avoid his table. The teacher on duty filed the queue in from left to right and from back to front. As it got nearer to Concord's table people would drop out of the queue and move back to a better place. It got so bad that the queue halted because everyone was reluctant to go in.

In the end the teacher on duty started to alternate the pattern so that the queue sometimes went in back to front, sometimes not. He would suddenly aim the queue at Concord's table before we could react. The teachers knew all about Concord, they did nothing. Inaction. We were children, they were professional teachers.

Every Friday we bought our lunch vouchers for the next week with a cheque from our parents. Every Monday I would queue to redeem them for cash, all of them. Just to avoid the horror of the dining hall. I did this for years and it was always the same teacher. It was his job to organise lunch vouchers. He never once questioned me over the course of several years.

Concord was actually the one who was doing the teaching, his subject was not Geography, it was life. The lesson was a powerful one. We all learned it. We learned of our insignificance, we were nothing, we were alone, a group of individuals, what could we do? What do we teach our children?

We merely teach them how to survive within the Hive. From a very early age we exhort them to struggle, to compete and improve. Already the child feels that he is not enough, inadequate. The seeds of Self loathing are planted. He is driven further into the cul de sac of competition, struggle and conflict. He feels he must improve, be the best and conceal any weakness. He will even create conflict, creating opportunity for advancement or to conceal himself from perceived threats to imaginary vulnerability. It is astonishing that we should treat young children in this way.

This process of conflict begins partly in the evolutionary process that has formed us, survival of the fittest, and partly in the way that we reinforce this instinctive behaviour. We teach our children that life is conflict, that they must strive to improve to overcome and conquer.

Who must we conquer? Our fellow humans, those who would use resources that we need. This is the purely biological Hive mentality. We

...e part of the family unit, the Tribe, society. All the while
...lf and elevating ourselves within the Tribe and against
...es. We learn all the tricks, manipulation, the art of lying and now to deceive. All the necessary evils we become attached to.

We love our babies but their cloistered, adored introduction to life is short lived. We soon begin the business of preparing them for the life we have created for ourselves. Qualifications, career, chores, work, materialism, more, more, more.

Further and further we travel away from the nurturing roots of God's love. We seek consolation in worldly things, mere distractions become our life's work. We ignore God's love and our own responsibility because we are not taught about Spirituality. We are not taught about Self. Some of us may receive an introduction to religion which can be a starting point. Most these days are not exposed to even this. At least religion can provide a moral code of behaviour which may lead us to explore our Spirituality.

God's Love has become an ineffectual cliché. It seems to be powerless in the face of our perceived reality. We ignore God and our true Selves living like wild animals. Our beliefs are not really beliefs, we do not consider or reflect on what we believe, we are too busy. Our so-called beliefs are merely what is acceptable to the community we live in, they are often hand me downs. They become so diluted with each generation that they are hardly relevant at all any more. Religion is becoming redundant. Our beliefs do not have any bearing on how we live our lives and when things go wrong we rush to God and blame him when he seems to turn his back.

Each of us is a potential triumph or disaster depending on how we live our lives. When we deny ourselves we perpetrate an individual sin, collectively these individual tragedies effect every aspect of modern life. The basic building blocks of society, people, are crippled, deformed. Our greatest resource is squandered, worse it is turned to the dark side perpetuating the cycle of chaos and misery.

It is true that life is an arena but we must teach our children that the real enemies are ignorance, intolerance, and fear. Not who, but what. We must fight these things in ourselves first and then in others. The true fight is in the understanding, educating and control of Self. It is time, not just as the odd individual, but as a society that we used our dynamic drive and love of conflict against the things that matter. In so doing we give our lives meaning and fulfilment.

By the time we reach a stage in our lives where we begin to question the established order we have already created a labyrinth of Self deceit around ourselves. Fear dominates our lives. Fear of being different, of being alone, of being wrong. Who are we to be different? We find it hard to believe in ourselves. Worse we have no respect or love for ourselves.

To begin to extricate ourselves we must admit that we have spent years going in completely the wrong direction. This is a very difficult thing to do. We must shout into the darkness of our Souls,
" Is anybody there?" Before we shout we must be prepared for an answer, a whimper from the encompassing gloom, or the silence of bitter pain and suspicion. It will not be pretty after what it has endured. How could it be? We are all traumatised, brutalised.

We are judgmental, we see things in terms of success or failure. We are hard on ourselves because we have little compassion for others and none for ourselves. Wherever you have been, whatever mistakes you have made, they have somehow brought you here, as a Seeker. There is hope.

The Universal Consciousness loves us without reservation. Allah, God, Jehovah, Buddha, take your pick, love is the common theme. Without it our lives are a desert whatever we believe. The love of a Mother for her child, the love between a man and a woman, husband and wife. The love of a child, the love of God. What do we have without it? Mere existence, and that, my friend, is not enough.

God loves us without reservation or qualification or limits. No matter what we have done or how low we think we have sunk. As a parent loves a child and beyond, so God loves us. He makes a distinction between us and what we do. He has to watch us getting it so wrong, hurting others and ourselves, unable to intervene, even when we blame him. We have the right and the responsibility to determine our own fate. This is Eden's terrible Legacy. God loves us to distraction and to his eternal pain, anguish and joy.

The problem is that we do not believe it. How could it be true? Look at us, look at me. To realise this Truth we need to find the child within ourselves, something that we can relate to and love. The being within that we can finally recognise as we would our own child.

As a baby your parents kissed your toes and doted on your every gurgle. The contents of your nappy were a serious matter of concern. No trouble was too great, no task too onerous. You accepted all of this as your right, which it was, blissfully ignorant of the trials ahead. Your confidence knew no bounds. Life was sweet and full as a sun kissed peach.

So what the hell happened? Well that's a long story isn't it? We could fill libraries with that one. My point is that whatever was done, was done to that child, you, over the course of the next few decades. There are choices but essentially the child is a victim of survival of the fittest mentality, our society's barbarism towards anything remotely unique. Somehow the child must survive all of this and undo all that has been done, heal the damage, try to understand the process and go on to help those behind.

This staggering task is to physically, mentally and Spiritually survive. Not only to survive but to understand, to evolve and ultimately achieve individual Salvation and to strive for the Salvation of all humanity. We are talking about you here, this is your job. So for goodness sake cut your Self a little slack, this is tough!

Imagine your Self as a child bleeding in the dust. Pick up the child with love and compassion, without thought, pick her up and hold her close. Feel the tears and let her cry, kiss the pain away, still her sobbing heart and let the child rest on your shoulder until she is ready to go on. Feel the compassion, let it grow, channel it towards that baby that is your Self, beneath a mountain of pain and suffering.

You have earned it, you deserve it.

It is important that you retain this image of your Self and reacquaint your Self with this neglected child. It is not an easy task, take some time and do it properly. Keep that picture of you as a child handy so that you can remind your Self.

For those of you who have no such memories or pictures you care to keep, remember, God loves you even though you do not feel loved or loveable. You perhaps most of all, touch Him deeply, imagine His pain as he is forced to watch you suffer. Even you, the most deserving must assume your burden of responsibility. None can save you except your Self. Throw off the bitterness, fear, anger and blame, begin to seek your own Salvation, then and only then can He at last scoop you up. Try it and see for your Self. Take the first step for your Self and see him at last intervene.

Fortunately, God's love shines untarnished no matter what we do. The clouds of our Self deceit obscure the sun, they do not lessen it's gorgeous radiance. It is always there for when we finally choose to seek it. Until there are enough of us to influence society we must struggle alone or in small groups.

The journey to find Self is long and painful. All the things the Hive has taught us must be unlearned and rejected. It is a daunting prospect. Courage, strength, wisdom and compassion are required. All will be provided unstintingly through God's love to those who have the will to begin.

To accept this challenge is to expand your own consciousness and therefore to expand the Universal Consciousness. This is no selfish act, it is truly the final frontier without bound, limit or restriction. Where on earth do we begin such a staggering journey?

It begins with the still small voice. The nagging unease and dissatisfaction that so many of us feel. No matter how successful we are as the Hive measures things we can never be at peace until we recognise the futility of it all. It comes to us all sooner or later, that haunting question, that has plagued mankind since the dawn of time, why? To what purpose?

The Hive cannot answer because it does not think or reflect, we can. We choose to avoid the question but we do have the necessary skills to answer it for ourselves if we are brave enough. The problem is that the study of Self is difficult in its own right, it is also deeply discouraged by our peers. By its very nature it goes against the Hive, it is the search for individuality. The search for Self is a direct challenge to the Hive.

The rules of the Hive are enforced primarily through our own conditioning. We are afraid to be alone, isolated, different. The bird's cage is open but he will not come out. Better to suffer in the cage where things are familiar than take the risk. If he does leave he will try to return, again and again to the comfort of the familiar, back to the Hive.

Eden's Legacy

To give you an idea of the difficulties here are a few of the remedies that I feel should be seriously considered by anyone interested in understanding themselves and their conditioning.

Counselling, receiving and giving.
Psychotherapy
Anger and emotion management.
Coping with change.
Assertion skills.
Time management.
Meditation.

If you ran a business that was in trouble you would not hesitate to bring in the necessary expertise to sort things out. Your struggle to achieve Enlightenment and freedom from the Hive is much more important. I spent many years immersed in the corporate jungle and was exposed to the full range of courses available to the modern executive. There is a lot of cynical rubbish out there but the discerning student can find invaluable resources to help in the struggle against the Hive.

Even in the corporate world I was often the only person interested in going on these courses. My colleagues despised such wimpy displays of weakness and they never had the time. The inference was that I did not have enough to do. Indeed there were many courses that I did not attend because I felt intimidated. As a private individual you will encounter the same intimidation.

"What would people think if they knew I was going for counselling?"

"If I go on an anger management course people will think I beat my wife."

Once again your Hive self is the main problem not your peers. Be aware of it working within you and make a conscious decision to do it anyway. Exercise a little Spiritual independence if you feel able. If you find it too much use a little Hive camouflage and go on your course in privacy. Either way do not be put off, look at Tony Soprano. Use every tool and weapon you can lay your hands on just as the Hive has taught you.

Gabriel Deeds

As a species we must outgrow the Hive. Humanity needs to accept the individual's need and right to explore Self. The Self is the basic building unit for everything, it must be strong. This is the evolutionary strategy that must evolve from the Hive if we are to move on.

A pipe dream? Maybe, or perhaps an ideal, something to strive for. Struggle is necessary, the sword of Truth and Self must be tempered, but this suffering should not be in vain. Without purpose there is only chaos and pain, look around you! Suffering should be our teacher and should serve a purpose. Each one of us has a purpose. Simply and beautifully put in the dying words of Buddha to his disciples,

"Diligently seek your own Salvation."

So begin your search, but before you start lay the foundation stone. God, the Universal Consciousness, loves you, personally, without qualification regardless of what you have done or what you feel about your Self. There are no exceptions! You are precious to Him and he will help you. In the trials ahead remember this.

Resources, see also appendix 1 and 2.

Books – The Road Less Travelled
Movies – Good Will Hunting, My Fair Lady,

Chapter 7   What do you believe?

You would think that our beliefs would play a fundamental part in how we live our lives. They don't. We have vague ideas about what we believe, the thing is we are so busy living our lives that we do not give much thought to our beliefs. If pressed we tend to fall back on what we were brought up with. Which is probably merely what our parents were brought up with.

We regurgitate a mixture of religious dogma and semi superstitious hocus-pocus. The truth is we rarely take time to consider our beliefs and how they should dictate the pattern of our lives. Without conscious beliefs that have been tried and tested we are in limbo between the baboon and the sentient, neither one nor the other. Remember time is a finite resource, ultimately it will lead you to the one thing that you know and cannot avoid. You will die, nothing could be more certain. Believe that!

Forget religion, it's too distracting. Take a big step back, we are going to look at underlying, fundamental principles before we tackle the details.

It is obviously important that we reflect on our beliefs.

The majority of us would completely agree. Nodding like those little dogs in the back windows of passing cars. Not good enough! Challenge the statement, examine it closely, criticise it, modify it, repudiate it. I don't care if you disagree, just have an informed opinion. If we do not undergo a rigorous examination process the result will not touch us or motivate us as it must if it is to be a belief and not just a feeling.

A human being motivated by true belief is an awesome thing. Such a person can achieve literally super human objectives against any odds. The odds become irrelevant, immaterial, a trivial detail. Without such belief the odds are the only factor that we consider and so we don't start at all, or we are easily defeated.

George Washington, Joan of Arc, Winston Churchill, Emily Pankhurst, Christopher Columbus, Marie Curie, Ghandi, Confucius, Nelson Mandela, Captain Cook, Mother Teresa, Martin Luther King,

Mohamed, Buddha. The list reaches back into antiquity and will stretch to the far distant future. All people, like you and I, but driven by what they believed, not caring one jot for victory or defeat, consumed only by their belief.

Belief is empowering, belief is inspiring. Without exception all of the above could not have achieved as much as they did without the inspired assistance of their fellow human beings. Indeed, the inspiration of others is in itself, perhaps the highest objective of all. Through their example these great ones have activated and focused the beliefs of those around them. This well of belief that lies within each of us can be tapped not only by famous leaders, but by each of us as an individual.

If we were able to shake off this Hive need for leadership and lead ourselves, imagine the world we would live in. Imagine if we were able to provide our own example and take responsibility for our own destiny, without the need for great leaders. Imagine if each of us could tap our own well of belief and inspire one another.

No longer paralysed and dormant, waiting for a saviour, we would be magnificent. Not just occasionally, between heroes, but perpetually, a gargantuan up welling of personal Self belief, unimaginable, cosmic energy. This would represent a quantum leap, the next level of Human existence. Caveman to Universal Consciousness.

Someday all the lights will come on at the same time, individual beams, overlapping, inextricably connected, illuminating everything. The fulcrum point, upon which the very possibility of the whole glorious design hangs by a single, silver thread, is you. Yes, you. Without you, none of this can come to fruition. You are the basic unit for the construction of the whole fantastic edifice.

You have inestimable value in the perpetual struggle for Enlightenment. There can be no paradise, no Heaven, no Nirvana until you are in it. You have no idea how precious you really are, how you are loved and nurtured, in spite of your Self. The whole Universe is waiting for realisation to dawn in you, waiting for you to finally pick up your burden and begin to shine.

Believe in your Self.

Eden's Legacy

Our beliefs must be reflected in how we live our daily lives.

How can you believe something if it doesn't touch your life? To believe one thing and do another is to lie to your Self, to deny your Self. Based on your own experience and knowledge, is that a recipe for a peaceful and happy life? Let me hear you say it.

"No"

If you have not investigated your beliefs essentially you have none. Without beliefs your life will lack any objective or meaning. A pointless, meaningless, deeply unhappy, unfulfilled existence. That's why we are here, together in this book, we are sick of it! We want more!

In order to proceed we need to keep our minds open and avoid falling back on familiar dogmas rather than on new possibilities. If you believe in your Self or even the possibility that what I have said might be true, then you must act.

You must investigate for your Self. Your beliefs will materialise and grow over time. As you search so you will become a wiser stronger person. As you walk through the minefield cautiously test every step, take nothing for granted. Your belief in your Self will grow and you will be shown the way, even when you stray. You are no longer on the fence and you can never return to sitting on it.

Accept what you are, you cannot waste any more time,

Seek the Truth.

As intelligent human beings we must now recognise what we do not know. We have the human archive to help us determine our own beliefs. We are looking for a system of beliefs that we can adapt to and adapt. We recognise the dangers and the difficulties and we will carefully analyse all the data at our disposal.

In this chapter I have divided our beliefs into,

1. What we were brought up with.
2. What we have experienced for ourselves.
3. What we conclude our beliefs are.

It is the process of investigation that is important rather than any specific beliefs that you might end up with. The important thing is how your honest beliefs affect the way in which you live your life. The person who lives in ignorance of their beliefs has some excuse no matter how flimsy. The person who has taken the trouble to investigate and does not act is in trouble.

I am not talking about hell fire and damnation, that's religion. Hell is here, all around us. Recognise the law of cause and effect. I believe that the effect of denying your Self is suffering, but you do not have to believe me, try it for your Self. You have already had a go at the suffering bit, try making it for the right reasons and avoid most of it completely.

What kind of fool professes a belief and does not live accordingly? Millions of us do just that, our beliefs, if we have them, are mere habit, a facsimile of belief. Our habitual belief allows us to don the uniform of acceptability, it is a tribal thing, a Hive thing. In the soft folds of this illusion we can hide from our own responsibilities.

This habitual belief does not task us with the difficult problem of how to love our neighbours or even ourselves. It has no substance, there is no challenge, only Self deceit and hypocrisy. It can be used by the Hive to create conflict that can and does last for thousands of years. Religious persecution is the kind of hateful, twisted irony that the Hive loves best. If you need more proof of Evil I am wasting my time. Cause and effect. You cannot disbelieve humanity's capacity for Evil, how can you doubt its capacity for Good.

There is ample evidence of humanity's capacity to do good collectively and individually. The existence of the two sides and the conflict between them is irrefutable.

Believe in the conflict between Good and Evil.

The vast majority of us these days are not practicing any form of traditional religious belief. Small wonder, we look at the glory that is Islam and see only a portrayal of Jihad and hatred, or Christianity, which is becoming synonymous with child abuse and sexual deviancy. The expression Allah Akbar has become a war cry and Jesus Christ an oath.

Eden's Legacy

The established religions seem ill equipped to deal with the looming problem of their own redundancy. Worse, millions of almost feral children have had not even the slightest contact with any religion. Their own Spirituality is unknown, untapped. They have no concept of faith or belief, it is not a part of their culture or their experience. Do not think for one moment that I am talking about the so-called Third world. Go to any city or town in the affluent West and you will see plainly who I am talking about.

Their religion is Nike, Snoop Doggy Dog and Microsoft. Their culture is to look after number one or me and my crew, dog eat dog. This bleak environment serves to provide the illusion of belonging to one faction or another. Anything but be without a tribe. It dulls the pain of unfulfilled existence, it provides another form of oblivion. In this respect it is just as valid as habitual religion They have no example of how a strong moral code can free them from suffering, they have no concept of their own Spirituality and worth.

Without clearly established beliefs and appropriate life styles we have no objective, no goals. We have only the deeply unsatisfying cocktail of tribalism combined with material and physical gratification which so dominates our lives. Millions of us live in debt, working too hard alongside neighbours we neither know nor wish to know. Addiction, poor mental and physical health and a deep-seated unhappiness are the hallmarks of our society.

This is the basic motivation for examining your beliefs. If you believe that any of the above applies to you then begin your search. You are looking for something better, infinitely richer and more satisfying.

Begin with an open mind. If you have strong beliefs, even if you believe in nothing, put them to one side for now. Try and separate your Self from what it believes. Be prepared to look objectively at your beliefs and be prepared to modify, reject or confirm them in equal measure.

This requires courage and confidence and will take a considerable time. It is an ongoing process, as your consciousness expands so will your beliefs. The process is the important thing. It will expose your dogmas and your insecurity which is of course troubling, alarming even. You need to be honest, if your existing beliefs cannot stand a little scrutiny they need changing.

At this stage the question of religion does not even arise. Step back from religion and have a look at your own experience of Self and it's beliefs.

As you consider your Self do you believe that you have a soul? As a physical entity you have,

1. Physical presence
2. Emotions
3. Thoughts

You are not any of these three alone.

From the Hindu Nirvanashatkam six stanzas on Salvation, first stanza,

"I am neither the conscious nor the unconscious mind, neither intelligence nor ego, neither the ears nor the tongue, nor the sense of smell or sight, neither ether nor air nor fire nor water nor earth. I am consciousness and bliss. I am Shiva."

Most of us would say that our soul and mind are linked in some way. What is it that feels physical sensation, experiences hate, jealousy, and emotion? What thinks these thoughts? Part of our mind and it's thoughts are involved in the mundane part of our lives,
" Tonight I will stay in and watch a movie." Another part of our mind, let us call it the Higher mind for now, provokes, questions, goads the lower mind into trying to justify and understand itself.
"Why am I?" It asks all the annoying questions, it is aware of it's Self and of it's coexistence with the rest of creation. It sees the systematic beauty and order of creation, its complexity and incredible sophistication, it wonders.
" How can this be?" This Higher Self seems to be in tune with the Universe. Like a child it picks up questions from school and brings them home to plague Mum and Dad.
" Where did Grandpa go when he died Mummy?"
What is this Higher Self that is making all this fuss? Is it our intellect alone? Can my intellect generate the question or is it just the

means to analyse the answer? Did the question come from another part of me separate from my intellect? Call it for now my Soul. Does this Soul exist outside my physical form or is it completely dependent on my body? Does it exist at all? Where is it finding all these awkward questions? Who has it been talking to?

Does this Self exist only in my mind or as part of creation, are they connected? What about everyone else, are we connected to each other as part of creation? Then there is the big question, where did this Self come from, is there a creator behind all this? We are aware of our Self and again we begin to wonder.

Please do not be so naïve as to expect an answer from me. This disturbing process is for each of us to undergo and evaluate. You are the only one that can answer for your Self. There are as many answers as there are sentient people, all equally valid. I will make so bold as to state that there is something within us beyond the physical and emotional. The question, is it Spiritual or intellectual is not important here. We have established the existence of what I call Self.

Your experience of your Self is real, fact.

Self is completely unique, it exists apart from humankind and religion, connected but apart. It is not just physical, emotional or entirely intellectual. Whatever it is it is the culmination of our evolution, the pinnacle of our existence. It should be the driving force in our lives, surely?

The physical Self is born alone, briefly. Then there is Mother, family, tribe, society. The connection with other Spiritual Selves is obliterated by the Hive. We are absorbed by it and must fight our way out of it. Like a rite of passage, somehow we must rediscover Self through our suffering. We must be reborn. Self is alone, a seedling growing slowly in the darkness of the Hive. As it develops it seeks understanding and companionship. It sees the majesty of the stars, the seasons turning and feels part of a greater order but cannot understand the connection.

Through what it feels, through what it needs and through the logic of it's intellect religion is born. This process applies to the Bushmen of the Kalahari or to any group of people at any point in time. Which religion is largely a question of birth. There has been religion for as long as people have wondered. They come and they go.

As soon as we come up with a religion it becomes entangled with our Hive beliefs and our biological conditioning. We seem to be unable to make the jump from primate to Spiritual being. Although often distorted, what progress humanity has made so far is contained in religion. It has great value as a resource if it is treated cautiously.

It is valuable both in the truth contained within it, but also as a survival tool for the fragile sentient. Communion, sharing a common belief, is a soothing balm to the troubled seeker of the Truth. In his voyage to Australia the great explorer, Captain Cook, had some charts from a previous expedition. As he crept through the labyrinth of the Great Barrier Reef, it became clear that some of the charts were real and some were pure fiction.

Cook knew this from bitter experience. The crew unaware of the poor quality of the charts followed Cook. Had they realised that the charts were full of mistakes they may well have mutinied and been destroyed on a hostile shore. So the chart, i.e. religion, is a potentially useful resource. Both as a guide, when treated with a pinch of salt, and as a buffer from a sometimes overwhelming Truth.

Consider that nowadays we fly to Australia in less than a day. The Great Barrier Reef is a place where we go on holiday. What would Cook have made of that? Sometimes an unreliable chart is better than no chart at all. Who can say where these dodgy old charts can take us if we are careful? They are not rigid codes to be followed slavishly, suppressing Self or for creating conflict as we so often use them. They are there to help us discover ourselves not to be worshipped in themselves.

We all seem to possess a basic need to believe in something greater than ourselves. Is this need an innate Spiritual awareness, a derivative of our own Soul? Does it come from a supreme Being, a Universal Consciousness? Or is it a combination of the two, push and pull with religion as a bridge connecting the two? Perhaps religion is the guidance we need to survive the right of passage and find the Path?

Or is it merely our own intellect railing at the possibility that we are indeed alone, doomed to die and be forgotten? Perhaps in a few thousand years we will have outgrown our physical form and all will be revealed by science. It is for each of us to make the effort to examine whatever options we can come up with and to go boldly forward. We must Captain our own ship and decide what is true and what is false.

Begin with your own religion if you have one. Accept it for what it is, a guide, it is not the only path to Salvation. I was in my thirties before I took the trouble to read the Bible. I had spent so many boring hours in church as a child that it never occurred to me to read it like I would any other book.

With the benefit of my experience as an adult much of what I read made a lot of sense. I threw out my old preconceived ideas about religion and I read about a man who suffered as I suffer. I felt a poignancy, a connection, a gentle passion and compassion for me and for my condition. He felt that I was important, and gradually I came to believe it my Self. I saw things from a different perspective, I saw my potential and my responsibilities.

I also read the Koran, the Bhagavad Gita and studied the writings of Buddha and the Dalai Lama. It struck me that our religions are very similar in some important respects. They all recognise the importance of the afterlife and provide a solid moral code for living so that we might attain "Heaven". As you study them and as your store of knowledge grows so you will outgrow the need for any particular one. You may have a favourite, perhaps the one you were brought up with, but you will realise that they are all compatible, equally valid.

The awareness of Self, sentience, arrives at a different time with every individual. Sometimes early, sometimes never. For each person the experience is different. It is often a mixture of dissatisfaction, suffering, lack of meaning and a strange awareness of their own importance. The Self emerges over the course of years, decades. The understanding of it and its control and purpose has been the subject of intensive study throughout the ages.

It is the first step that is truly important. The vague awareness, the uneasy and frightening realisation of Self must be translated into an action. A single step forward instantly transports the individual into something else. The suffering, slave becomes a soldier in the ranks of all those Spiritual warriors who have gone before. The first step may be tiny, a visit to the library or a quick search on the Internet. If it is truly the dawning of Self and the search for peace and happiness, you will succeed.

For those of you that remain unconvinced, consider your present life. Are you content? Do you want something better? Then all that is required is that you try. What could be more interesting than your Self? What have you got to lose? What is holding you back?

The emerging sentient should realise the value of Self and also the difficulties and responsibilities now ahead. It is important to remain independent and responsible for our own Self but at the same time to realise that help is available for so important a task. Indeed it seems clear that those more advanced along the Path progress only by helping those behind. This common theme of Self sacrifice permeates most religious teachings. It is also clear that you cannot sacrifice your Self until you have mastered it and owned it.

Although we must be Self reliant we must also be wise in our choice of tools. If we are to advance we must be aware of what we do not know and carefully select guidance from those who know more. Alone it is hopeless, even dangerous, we shrivel and quickly shirk the task which can be so overwhelming. We need each other.

So we are now aware of our mutual dependence.

We cannot go on alone without the teaching and support of others more experienced while they cannot progress without us. As we struggle to learn we gain knowledge and become aware of those toiling behind us in ignorance and suffering. Their suffering is our suffering for we have been where they are now. They are no longer competitors but brothers and sisters and so we go back to help. We are drawn by the bonds of common suffering to help them and the final irony is disclosed. In so sacrificing Self to help others we save ourselves.

Conclusion

1. It is important that we investigate our beliefs.
2. Our beliefs must be reflected in how we live our daily lives.
3. We are mutually dependent on our fellow human beings.

You know this to be true. You have always known it to be true. Your life is a mess because you refuse to fight for what you know to be true. What do you expect? It is not enough to not be Evil, you must actively fight for Good. This is hard and dangerous, it requires sacrifice and pain. Pain we are good at, anyone would think that we enjoyed it. The cursed thing that stops us is our fear of being alone and our ignorance of how to start. Our Hive training leaves us in need of leadership.

This is what cripples us, we wait for a Messiah, someone to save us. Look what happens when we find one! The starting point whether for Good or Evil is always an individual, an example, a leader. The terrible unavoidable truth is that we must each of us lead ourselves, we cannot affords to wait on the sidelines. Stop looking over your shoulder at what everyone else is doing.

It is your job to realise your Self, nobody else can or will do it for you.

This is a responsibility we would rather avoid even at the cost of our own peace and happiness. There are numerous examples of how to save your Self, any good religion will show you how. The next section of this book might help, the only thing that matters is that you begin. We all want peace, happiness and Salvation, but no one is going to just give it to you. You must understand the conflict, feel it in your heart and your guts. Choose a side, choose to live your life accordingly.

This is why we seek oblivion in career, chemicals and chaos. We prevaricate and distract ourselves in a thousand ways. They are all ultimately negative and cause suffering. We must pick up the gauntlet, not in the heat of battle, proud and defiant, but quietly, resolutely, more than a little afraid, seeking help carefully and with compassion for ourselves and others. Accept the challenge of establishing your Beliefs and your objective, the saving of your Self.

"Diligently seek your own Salvation." (Buddha)

"Seek and ye shall find." (Jesus Christ)

"Salvation is promised to the believer; but he is at the same time bound to abstain from Evil, and to do good works." (The Koran)

"Those who realise the Self are always satisfied. Having found the source of joy and fulfilment they no longer seek happiness from the external world." (Bhagavad Gita)

Gabriel Deeds

Resources, see also appendix 1 and 2.

Books – Nelson Mandela (autobiography).
Movies – Ghandi, Hurly Burly.

Chapter 8   Success, a new definition

We are constantly measuring our own performance and that of those around us. Our friends, our family our workmates, even strangers, everyone we meet has to be assessed and pigeon holed. How are we doing? Is the other person bigger, better more successful? Competition pervades our lives, we swim in it like fish in the sea.

Sometimes we see ourselves as superior, sometimes inferior depending on circumstances but also largely depending on how we perceive ourselves. This Self perception is at the root of all our woes and troubles. The Hive is conflict, survival of the fittest. It seems we are always looking for trouble so that we can measure ourselves. If we were all relaxed and confident about our Self worth there would be no conflict. There would be nothing to prove, no contestants.

In the biological, evolutionary context, this would be disastrous since it is the conflict that provides the driving force of natural selection. The Hive does not care if we are unhappy! It cares only that we should crush the enemy, compete and reproduce.

We are so used to projecting an image of ourselves, to give us a competitive edge, that we have lost touch with the real person. The image becomes our objective, and the image is controlled by the Hive. We seldom perceive ourselves as others do and almost never as we really are. This is a sad reflection of the mess that we are in. The real Self is lost and we are not even sure if we want to find it.

Reality and perception overlap, the edges blur and the two seem to merge. Our hasty ill conceived thoughts are actually nothing more than instincts and learned responses. Our so-called thinking is corrupted by experience and our conditioning and creates actions which have real consequences. These realities are based on a biological system of competitive evolution more suited to baboons than people.

Yet we allow these seemingly overwhelming realities to dictate the pattern of our lives. We are ever reactive not proactive. How in God's name could we be happy living like this? Here is an example,

A young man applied for a job and was surprised when he got it. He was worried, out of his depth. He moved away from his family and friends to the big city and bought a house. As a senior manager he had to attend meetings, he was always a bit overawed by the suits and the jargon. Never the less he quickly learned the jargon, bought a couple of suits and took his lead from the boss who, unfortunately, was a bad tempered, mean old bastard.

The young man realised that nobody bothered the boss with awkward questions or tasks because he attacked everybody that came to his attention. Soon the young man was just as mean and bad tempered and was promoted to an even more high powered job. He was successful. He had to provide monthly accounts for the boss and present them at the meetings. The young man sweated seventy hours a week to try and make the figures look good, but the figures were just too bad. At the meetings the young man was savagely attacked by the boss and then by all his workmates, people that he himself had attacked many times before.

The next month he worked even harder to try and sort out the figures. He became really desperate. He was exhausted, he had high blood pressure and terrible headaches. In a moment of blind panic he made up the figures just to get through the next meeting. All he wanted was to survive the meeting, he would worry about being found out later.

At the meeting he presented the figures and the boss was delighted with him. His workmates were delighted as well and soon he was being invited to sit in on various projects and committees. He was a big cheese again. Now the young man was terrified that the truth would come out and that he would be disgraced. Weeks went by, months, the young man just produced whatever figures he thought would please the boss and everyone was happy.

The young man was beginning to feel guilty, his headaches continued and he became sick. He put on a lot of weight and was tired all the time. He still worked seventy hours a week because being sick was not allowed. Being sick was a sure way of getting attacked by the boss and of course by everybody else. He was driving a new company car, he had an expense account and a fat salary, success.

At the next meeting the boss was so pleased that he announced that his chief accountant was bringing a team down to see just how the young man managed his department so well. Horrified the young man redoubled his efforts to massage the figures but he knew that the accountant would spot the obvious deception. Eventually he collapsed at work and was taken to hospital. The doctors told him he was suffering from high blood pressure and exhaustion and that he was in grave danger of dying from a heart attack. He went home in a daze resigned to his fate. He told everyone at work that he had a viral infection and that everything was OK.

Eventually the accountant arrived and the young man took him through all the figures that he had concocted with a heavy heart. The two men liked each other and several times he found himself on the point of telling the accountant the truth. After a couple of days the accountant took all his figures away and said that it would take a week for his report to be ready. The young man was thinking about just running away or even killing himself.

The report arrived and a copy was sent to the boss. To his astonishment the report was very complimentary and he was promoted again. He spoke to the accountant and the accountant laughed and laughed and laughed. He told the young man that the mean old bastard was almost illiterate, completely out of his depth. He wasn't a mean old bastard at all, he was just terrified of the younger generation of managers. He knew the job could not last and was simply taking whatever he could get before the game ended.

Gradually realisation dawned, the young man knew with complete certainty that nobody actually cared about the facts and the figures, nobody actually read his accounts. Nobody wanted to upset the boss and everybody was doing exactly the same as he was, they were making it up. Suddenly he could see what a fool he had been.

Shortly after he resigned and moved to another job. Ironically, he sold his house and it had doubled in value since he bought it. The house, sitting doing nothing for two years had made much more money than he had sweating and suicidal at work. The young man was appalled at his own foolishness and the pain and suffering that he had endured apparently for no reason. Twelve months later his old company went into liquidation.

Our suffering seems all too real, it is brought about by our own inability or unwillingness to think about our lives and how we live them. We wander from crisis to crisis without any clear idea of what we are doing or where we are going. We are always reacting to the illusory minutiae, caught up in the Hive's perception of success rather than thinking and planning the important things in life.

The fact is that in the Hive's game there is always someone we see as better. Even if we make it to the top of the pile, we can't stay long, someone "better" always comes along. This is the nature of our biological evolution, it is a struggle for supremacy. A little healthy competition can be a useful motivator, it's in our nature to strive and compete, this is not the problem. The problem is our perception of success and the parameters we use to measure it. We need to examine our objective, set some goals and create the proper means to measure our performance.

This is not rocket science, this is a technique we commonly use for problem solving in work situations. It is a Hive technique, but we never apply the same skills to our lives. The fact is we have become so accustomed to projecting the successful illusion of our perceived lives that this has become our objective.

The Hive is a master bullshitter. If it looks like the other guy has the edge, make something up, fake it. This is one of the underlying principles of our lives. It's a commonly accepted truism that the biggest bullshitters get the best jobs. I'm talking politics here. From the frog that sucks in air to make itself look bigger to the Presidential motorcade.

When the frog starts trying to convince himself that he is big and powerful trouble is not far off. We cannot pretend to be what we are not and expect to find any kind of peace in this life. Instead because we know deep down that we are pretending, lying, we begin to despise ourselves. At the same time we desperately wear ourselves out competing in a foolish game that cannot be won. In so doing we also destroy are mental and physical health. Cause and effect.

We need to feel successful, fine, but when we lack objectives, when we are not on the right path, when as a consequence we are filled with deep Self loathing, we over compensate. We desperately struggle to maintain the illusion of success in its commonly accepted form. We fall back on our survival of the fittest conditioning. We lose sight of the objective and strive only to impress others rather than for our Selves.

More money, bigger house, better job, bigger muscles, stronger, faster, more beautiful, slimmer, younger, better educated, more responsibility, more power, more connections. On and on and on. We try

Eden's Legacy

to convince others of our success to conceal our vulnerability and to distract ourselves from the reality of our miserable condition. Surely if we can succeed in these terms we will win?

I remember once as a child my Teacher asked me to write out the numbers one to ten. I couldn't do it, or rather it was too much trouble. I noticed above the blackboard the entire alphabet was laid out in individual letters. Laboriously I copied the entire alphabet into my book and raised my hand, very smug. This was after all much more impressive than the first ten numbers, wasn't it? No it was not! My Teacher made me stay behind and do my numbers.

This is how we live our lives, striving for the wrong things, denying the more onerous task of saving ourselves. Ironically we suffer far more in this way than if we just got on with it. The difficult thing is in making "it" a tangible thing, something we can identify and tackle.

We do not have the luxury of having someone to force us to do what we should be doing. We have free will, Self determination, sentience, Eden's terrible legacy. We are responsible, not the Universal Consciousness, not God, us! There are hints and glues and help everywhere. God plays an endless game of charades with us bending over backwards to try to get us to see the Truth. He leaps through every hoop we can produce and we carry on stumbling about like imbeciles. We even blame him for all our woes, desperately trying to hand back the responsibility that is our birthright.

I read somewhere that if you took ten thousand chimpanzees and gave them a typewriter each sooner or later one of them would turn out War and Peace. Imagine how it would feel to stand there and watch them waiting for it to happen. Imagine the frustration, the temptation to help. This is what God has to put up with from humanity. Patiently waiting for the penny to drop.

Like any Father he gets angry and frustrated. He may punish us or help us when we allow it but he never ignores us as we ignore him. He loves us. Imagine his pain. Think about what happens daily in our world. Murder, rape, child abuse, genocide, ethnic cleansing, famine. God has to watch all this, waiting for us to get it right.

When it dawns on you how much even your thoughts can hurt Him, when He becomes as real to you as a member of your own family you will naturally change your life. Even if you do not believe in a God, how long can you live like this? How unhappy do you need to be before you do something? Do it for your Self.

So how do we know when we are doing it right? How do we know what "it" is? How do we measure success in this strange conflict?

You will find a fully worked out action plan in chapter 15. Very task orientated, very Hive. Use the skills the Hive has taught you. The process is the same but you will find the objective and goals very alien indeed. Meanwhile, here are some thoughts on how different real success is compared to our twisted perception of it.

Happiness

We all want to be happy, I don't think anyone on the planet would argue that people have a right to seek happiness. Even our worst enemies deserve the chance to seek happiness. How many of us achieve that goal? Very few, very few indeed. The problem is simple, how can you find something when you have no clue what it is.

Once again we fail to reflect on the subject and tear straight into the doing bit. Sex drugs and rock and roll, and of course, money. All the things that we think will make us happy. Happiness is relative to our physical, emotional and mental condition. As such it is a moving target, sometimes we get a taste, but it is never enough. We always overlook the fourth element, our Spirituality.

We may feel happy after a good work out or after good sex. Even better a romantic dinner and good sex with someone we love. Physical, emotional and mental happiness, yes, temporarily and depending almost entirely on what chemicals are present in our systems. Adrenaline, endorphins, alcohol and hormones, a lethal, volatile cocktail. We are like demented alchemists constantly playing with the formula trying to turn lead into gold. Many among these unhappy chemists settle in the end for an absence of pain, anaesthesia as an alternative to happiness. They discover all too late that the price is addiction, despair and death.

This "happiness" is transient and unfulfilling in the long term. We are addicted to short term gratification of our senses, we are forever trying to recreate little moments of so called happiness. It doesn't work, take a look around you, take a look at your own life. True or false?

Your body will let you down especially as you get older. Your emotional happiness is a roller coaster and mental happiness is unattainable because your mind is aware of your suffering. Happiness is an illusion that tortures us like a mirage in the desert, stop chasing it. What you are after is not happiness at all, it is peace.

"Those who realize the Self are always satisfied. Having found the source of joy and fulfilment they no longer seek happiness from the external world. They have nothing to gain or lose by any action; neither people nor things can affect their security."

The Bhagavad Gita

Peace

"Responsibility does not only lie with the leaders of our countries or with those who have been appointed or elected to do a particular job. It lies with each of us individually. Peace, for example, starts within each one of us."

His Holiness the Dalai Lama.

Peace is a different animal altogether. It grows from understanding and compassion, from discipline and hard work. Peace is pervasive, durable and satisfying in a way unknown to most of us. It is a way of life, a way of living and best of all we can learn how to achieve it.

Peace comes to us somewhere along the true Path as a by-product of our search for Salvation. That journey begins when we accept our plight, when we recognise what has been done to us and what we have learned to do in the name of the Hive. When you have suffered enough and when you recognise the conflict that is your life, when you seek something better.

At this point you will not feel successful, but you are. Your pain and your growing sentience bring you exhausted and bleeding to the Threshold of Knowing. At this point your subconscious knowledge of the lie that is your life can be expressed in your waking consciousness. You can finally see your life for what it is, a fabrication.

This is not just a success, it is a triumph.

This is true success but it is unrecognised by the Hive and even by those who achieve it. They are so injured and broken that they do not see the victory and worse, much worse because they cannot see the way ahead or even suspect its presence they merely feel failure. The Hive has crushed them and drives their broken souls back to the salt mine which is their life.

So where is this success? It is in your growing awareness. Whatever you have endured has brought you to this place, the Threshold of Knowing. You are aware of your injured Self and the conflict between Good and Evil. You are aware of your own responsibility and the role you must play in your own Salvation. At last you can see the world as it truly is, you can see through the Hive's elaborate illusion and your own fear.

"These two paths, the light and the dark, are said to be eternal, lending some to liberation and others to rebirth. Once you have known these two paths, Arunja, you can never be deluded again." (The Bhagavad Gita).

This Self awareness will turn to growing Self confidence and a deep desire to learn and understand and to help others in the struggle to achieve their own awareness. To fully realise your success you must cross through the Threshold of Knowing and begin to take the first steps on the Path to Enlightenment.

Two words of caution,

1. To achieve this awareness and not to act is to turn victory into defeat and endure further suffering.
2. Reflect and meditate, remember thought is action in its purest form.

Beware of doing!

So how do you cross through and begin? These are just words, you need practical help. If you are to utilise your Hive skills and intelligence we need something more tangible. Your first success was in realising that the conflict exists, now what? Our first response is often to do something. We join a Church or become a volunteer serving soup to the homeless. Straight in without thinking as we have been taught.

The next success is in realising that you come first. Before you can help anyone you must help your Self. We are very bad at doing nothing because it is when we are still, unoccupied, that our inner voices make themselves heard. We have been trained to blot them out in activity, even charitable deeds can distract us. At this point you are extremely vulnerable you must have a specific template to follow until things crystallise in your mind. For now, when you are ready, follow the action plan in chapter 15.

Now is anybody else interested in you or you personal happiness? Is anybody else trying to help you through this? I bet not another soul on the planet knows what you are going through right now. That's true, it has to be that way but I am trying to help. Why I hear you say.

Well we have established that we all want happiness, we have also established the fact that happiness is a trap and what we really want is peace. I want peace. I am a lovely person and I deserve to be at peace, the Universe loves me, God loves me, he wants me to have peace, but he won't just give it to me. I have to be smart enough to want it and smart enough to know how to attain it for my Self. It's my responsibility to earn it.

The Universe, God, doesn't just want me but you as well, all of us. So I can earn my ticket to paradise by helping you.

There is no other way.

So for better or worse friend, we are stuck with each other. You hold the key to my peace and happiness. Remember that the same applies to you, as a species we are all mutually dependent on each other. This is a common theme that runs throughout many of the world's religions, it's not just me ranting on.

Start with your Self, you don't need to believe in any greater power. It is self evident that within each of us there is a seed of Divinity something deeply troubling and unfathomable. In some way we are connected to the Universe and it can and does drive us crazy. Frankly life would be a lot easier without it. If we really were just like sheep instead of pretending to be like sheep we wouldn't be plagued by this knowledge that I call Eden's Legacy. Just one thing though, do you really want to be a sheep?

It's not that you want to be a sheep its that you simply do not know how to handle this terrifying responsibility. This realisation that you are indeed a truly special person and that as a super being you have heavy responsibilities. Success is realising this fact and dragging it out into the sunlight. Throw it on the table, recognise your own true Self and marvel at its shimmering beauty and fabulous worth. When you are ready and in possession of your Self, then and only then, you can think about doing.

At this point religion is irrelevant, this is pre-religion, pre-anything. This is the first hesitant step on a life long journey of exploration on the only frontier that really matters. This first step is like the launching of a great ocean liner, there should be bands playing and crowds of well-wishers cheering, fireworks, celebration and jubilation.

I believe that there are, that all of Heaven will celebrate your first step. How do I take it? Stop beating about the bush I hear you say. **You already have**, that is the purpose of this book. In reading it and in searching you have begun. The greatest victory of all is won in your own mind, as you begin the process of achieving Enlightenment. Where you go now and what you ultimately believe is for you to investigate and decide.

Measure success in terms of what you know and what you understand, in terms of how aware you are.

1. Be aware of the conflict and suffering that is your life.
2. Be aware of your own worth, love your Self.
3. Be aware that the Universe/God loves you.
4. Be aware of your responsibility for your own Salvation.
5. Be aware of your interdependence on your fellow humans.
6. Seek your own Salvation and live your life accordingly.

You will see a list forming as above. Remember the lists have all been done before. Its called religion. Check them out. You have already done the hard bit, now live the dream.

Resources, see also appendix 1 and 2.

Books – The New Testament, Destructive emotion, (the Dalai Lama.)
Movies – The Mission.

Section Three, chapters 9-13 Offence and defence.

Chapter Nine: Offence

1. Character
2. Discipline
3. Material resources

Chapter Ten: Assertion skills

1. Assertion
2. Personal Rights
3. How to assert your Self

Chapter Eleven: Self Defence

1. The enemy
2. The Threshold of Knowing
3. Counter measures

Chapter Twelve: Social Interaction, surviving it!

1. Pack instinct
2. Peer pressure
3. Relationships

Chapter Thirteen: The Body

1. The horse
2. Food and sleep
3. Sex

Chapter Fourteen: The Mind

1. Separation
2. Emotion
3. Thought

Chapter Fifteen: The Action Plan

1. Objective
2. Goals
3. Monitor and review

Chapter Sixteen: Conclusion

Chapter 9   Offence, the campaign

You have now completed section one, attempting to identify the enemy personified as the Hive and what it has done to you. This was by way of an intelligence analysis of the Hives capabilities and strength, they are impressive. You have also completed section two, your personal audit and beliefs. To proceed you must have a clear idea of what it is you are trying to achieve. This section deals with your plan of action. With a clear objective, personal fulfilment, it is now your task to marshal your resources and plan your campaign.

Some topics in the following sections fall into both offence and defence categories and so you may feel a sense of deja vu as you read.

Make no mistake, this is a conflict, one in which you can be crippled or destroyed if you decide to fight! Remember however that even if you don't fight you will be injured as a non-combatant. Depression, mental illness, addiction, frustration and deep unhappiness are wounds casually inflicted by the Hive. Your life as a slave will sooner or later become intolerable. You can break free and finally realise your own potential and in so doing find peace. All you have to do is try.

I often use warfare as a metaphor, one that we can easily relate to. This allows me to give the enemy form and use strategies and tactics more easily understood in this context. In this way I can bring the natural strengths of our organising, logical faculties into play.

This conflict is real, it is the enemy which is elusive, almost invisible. The effects of this conflict on us as individuals are devastatingly obvious. We suffer passively because we fail to marry cause and effect and are neutralised. We fail to understand the cycle of our own existence concentrating only on the illusory physical, emotional and intellectual aspects of our lives.

Our hearts and most of our minds are still in the jungle, our Higher mind and Spirit are ignored and neglected. We ignore or hide from the Divine within us and around us. We suffer as a result of our inability to accept responsibility for our Selves and to believe in our Selves.

I have so far in this book tried to identify the enemy within us. The Hive is like the Nazi party, it can only thrive if it can control the behaviour of the individual through ignorance and fear, through peer pressure. By understanding this and by openly discussing the nature of this conflict we put the spotlight onto a previously invisible enemy. Once identified we lack only the courage to be the first to stand up and resist. One thing is certain, we have ample opportunity to test ourselves.

The vast majority of us live like the Vichy French under Nazi occupation. The trains run on time the bread still gets baked, it's not so bad. Yes people disappear, but not me, yes I am scared, I don't go out, waiting for the knock on my door but I survive. At what cost?

The still small voice of our Self consciousness is the Resistance. The Universal power is the Allies dropping supplies and helping when it can. Suffering breeds discontent and frustration which in turn leads to thoughts of sedition. Thought is the precursor to action, small acts of resistance and finally open rebellion. The few, the many, the all. The enemy will be defeated.

Before we continue let us take stock of the weapons we have available to us. You will need to become familiar with each one and be proficient in their use. These weapons are difficult to master. Each one is a separate subject worthy of serious study. They will take time to master and will quickly become a real part of your life.

Remember always that they are a means to an end. If you decide to study Judo to improve your Self discipline, your objective is still personal Salvation, not to become a black belt. Do not confuse goals with your objective. This is a favourite Hive trick for the diversion of those whose vigilance fails them. That's all of us, sooner or later, by the way.

It is not my intention to repeat what has already been written regarding humanity's dilemma. The wisdom of the ages lies ready for you in a dozen formats. I seek only to bring you to an understanding of the reality of life's conflict and the inevitability of your eventual participation. By adding structure and form to a difficult and frightening subject I hope to encourage you to begin the search for Salvation. The end result will depend entirely on you, as it must.

These weapons or resources are subdivided into three headings,

1. Character
2. Skills
3. Material

Gabriel Deeds

Character

The resources found in good character are not numerous but without them you will never unlock the power of all the other resources available to you through the use of Self discipline. These character resources overlap and even merge together, that is fine, it is the blend that makes you.

Courage

"Fear is the Father of courage, her Mother is compassion."

Gabriel Deeds

Be brave, remember, courage is the control of fear not its absence. I can jump out of an aeroplane without a qualm. That is not brave for me since I enjoy it, but ask me to go into a room full of strangers and I'm off. What is courageous for one is fun for another. Without fear there can be no courage.

It is not wrong to be afraid it is only wrong to allow fear to prevent you from doing what you know to be right. The knowledge of what is right and wrong is a part of Eden's Legacy. If you allow your Self, give your Self time and opportunity to reflect and listen you will know. If you know, you must do what is right, for this you need courage.

The courage to act collectively, but especially the courage to act alone. Lack of belief in ourselves turns us into sheep. We are immobilised, constantly looking at the rest of the flock to see what they are doing. We are happy to be anonymous and out of the spotlight. At least you cannot be blamed or singled out when you are just one among many. Better to be wrong together than risk being right alone.

We are all guilty of it, but we are not born this way. The Hive makes us a herd animal because we are more manageable as bovine drones. It does this not by attacking our courage which would be a tactical blunder. The human race is capable of fantastic courage, the Hive is much more devious than that. It undermines our courage years before we need it. How?

Eden's Legacy

The key requisite for courage is confidence. Self confidence allows us to look our fear in the eye and roll up our sleeves. Low Self esteem and a lack of Self confidence sap our courage. We are neutered by our lack of belief in ourselves, we are made docile and obedient to the Hive. It takes a special, pure form of courage to act alone without any belief in your Self. It's called Faith. Believe in the Universal Power as evidenced by you. Self belief will come.

We are like a wife who has been systematically beaten by her husband for years. This is an all too common scenario. We all say why on earth doesn't she leave him? The answer is simple her Self confidence is gone. She will stick with the devil she knows because she does not believe that she can manage alone. Her fear, our fear overcomes us, we do not realise the power we possess.

Only a fool fears nothing. It is good to be afraid, healthy. Fear sharpens the mind, but courage is a finite resource. The bravest of us will buckle and break eventually if our courage is not replenished from the well of the Universe's love for us.

Even when we are broken and our courage fails us we can recover, we can be forgiven and begin again. We can be beaten, but never defeated. True, but better to avoid being beaten through realising that this is a long fight and that you must husband your courage wisely. Never take your courage for granted.

There is a direct correlation between what we are frightened of and what we are dishonest about. If you have the courage to list the things that frighten you, really frighten you, then you will have gone a long way to conquering your fear.

Honesty

It is important that you are honest, particularly with your Self, but also in your dealings with other people. You know your Self what is honest and what is dishonest, right and wrong. Have the courage to be honest, attune your thoughts to constantly monitor your actions. Take time to reflect on your daily activities and consider your motives before acting.

Dishonesty is something we are all guilty of. How have you been dishonest? Why are you dishonest? What can you do about it? I am not talking about a dubious expense claim or that money you forgot to pay back, it runs much deeper than that. Here are some examples of how we can be dishonest to get you started.

> Are you in a dead relationship?
> Are you being dishonest to your partner?
> Are you truthful about where you go and why?
> Are you honest at work?
> Are you happy at work or just going through the motions?
> Are you frightened to change things?
> How do you apportion blame to people, at home and at work?
> Do you say or think bad things about people without talking to them?
> Do you accept responsibility for your Self?
> Are you honest about your sexuality?
> Are you honest about your health?
> Are you honest about your habits?
> Are you lonely?
> Do you fear being alone?
> Do you fear old age?
> Do you fear death?
> What makes you feel guilty?
> Do you believe in God?
> What happens when you die?
> How does your belief effect your life?

Have the courage to ask the big questions and the honesty to answer. It is only when you admit how bad things are, that you can begin to repair the damage. Realising the Truth, being honest, no matter how painful, is a real success.

Independence

Remember that your own journey is unique. Mine and others may have similarities but remember you are enough by your Self. You must be prepared to stand out. Your Self has been immersed in the Hive for so long that you will fear being alone.

Be aware of how your thoughts and actions are modified by other people and organisations. A religious belief or an emotion, guilt for example, can modify our behaviour for better or worse. The Church might say you cannot wear a condom, on the other hand what about unwanted pregnancy and disease. It does not matter if you decide to use one anyway or if you decide to obey the Church, it matters only that you evaluate and decide for your Self.

You are not alone, you have direct access to the Love of the Universe through reflection and prayer. This personal relationship is the foundation upon which your Salvation will come about. Beware of slavishly following anyone or anything else, it is too tempting to follow and so abrogate responsibility for your Self.

Guru hunting, looking for a Saviour to make everything better, is a popular pastime. Those who are distracted from the Path and enmeshed in illusion find solace in cults only to be disappointed and led astray. Never give up your independence, remember that you are responsible for your own Salvation, nobody else.

Will Power

When you are beset by all the enemies and dangers listed further in this chapter remember that the greatest among them is you. That is, your Hive self. See the Hive self as separate from the real Self, it is subservient to the real Self. No matter how bold and strong and domineering it may seem it is afraid of you. You do not need the Hive to survive anymore only to hide behind. Once you gain the upper hand it is finished, because ironically it doesn't exist at all except in you and your behaviour. You are afraid of you, or rather what you might become should you dare to try.

Once you realise this, the Hive becomes redundant and the real you is exposed blinking, frightened and confused in the light of realisation. No matter what torture it puts you to or how hopeless it all seems you are greater than it and the Hive self must learn its place, your higher Self is master. This is true no matter how overwhelmed you may feel. The Hive can beat you, humiliate you and fill you with despair, but it cannot defeat you. That you have to do your Self.

However bad things seem remember you are the child of God beloved of the Universe. Put your troubles into perspective and carry on a little bit longer. Even if you feel you are at the end of your rope, continue anyway. Be unreasonable and stubborn even when the whole world seems to tell you how foolish you are. You will have to deliberately put your Self out of step with the rest of Humanity and dare to believe that you are right and they are wrong. Dare to believe in your Self.

Nobody but you can save you or destroy you. You alone have that power, you must believe this and find the will to do what is necessary to achieve victory. To win you only need to fight and not give up. This is in itself victory.

When you come to your dark place remember these words, you were expecting this, you are prepared for it. Even when you make mistakes, they are honest and genuine, they can and will be corrected. You absolutely will not stop, and further, even in your iron resolve you must be wary of arrogance and Self deceit. Do not be afraid to review your beliefs, we are not interested in dogma. Be sure and being sure do not be swayed. Do it your own way, find your own Salvation.

In the words of a great man, who knew about pain, conflict and will power,

"It is not the critic who counts, not the man who points out how the strong man stumbled, or where the doer of deeds could have done them better. The credit belongs to the man who is actually in the arena; whose face is marred by dust and sweat and blood; who strives valiantly, who errs and comes short again and again; who knows the great enthusiasms, the great devotions, and spends himself in a worthy cause; who, at the best, knows in the end the triumph of high achievement; and who at the worst, at least fails while daring greatly, so that his place shall never be with those cold and timid souls who know neither victory nor defeat."

Teddy Roosevelt

Skills

Objectivity

Recognise that the patient cannot always cure himself. Be objective, be vigilant. Given the damage that has been inflicted on you over the years will you be able to remain objective? Will you avoid all the distractions and pitfalls? Unlikely. Recognise that you will go astray falling back on old habits. Plan for that eventuality. You are not alone, you do have resources at your disposal.

Assume that you will naturally go astray, periodically review what you are doing in your search. How you have changed your thinking and your behaviour. Reflect with suspicion on all your actions since the greatest changes should be taking place in your head, not with your hands. Build this review into your structured regime, weekly or perhaps monthly.

Taoists believe in a doctrine of inaction. Not in doing nothing but of waiting for the perfect moment before acting. This is incredibly difficult for us. We tend to do it the other way around. We act before we think. We react to outside stimuli such as other people's opinions of us and our warped sense of success and how to achieve it. In so doing turn our lives into a labyrinthine mess that is convenient for avoiding the Truth. Stand back from your life and regard it as if you were looking at the life of a friend who needs help.

A third party may help you to achieve objectivity. It doesn't have to be a friend, in fact it is easier sometimes with a stranger. A trained councillor can be an invaluable aid to helping you understand and tease out your thoughts and actions. I can personally recommend it. Friends or family inevitably have a slant to whatever advice they give. It is not advice that you require but a sounding board for your own thoughts, a safety check to help you avoid delusion and keep you on the Path. Consider bringing in resources to help you in your struggle, try your doctor for a referral to a councillor. Use whatever you can find, unashamedly.

It took me a little while to come to terms with the concept but it helped me in many ways. I also quickly realised that the councillor was not a magician but a facilitator. The answers inevitably came from within me not the councillor. By setting time aside in a formal setting I created a threat free environment in which I could do some serious thinking about my life. It very quickly became apparent that one hour a week was simply not enough. I raised far more questions than answers. More and more of my time was required to consider what had happened to me and what I was now going to do.

I could return with my thoughts to the councillor who simply encouraged me to investigate and analyse them further. I realised that I could identify and solve all my own problems once I freed my Self to do the job. For me, that single hour every week was filled with spontaneous insight that kept me busy throughout the rest of the week. So much of my life was filled with actions that were the result of fear and anger brought on by an unconscious knowledge that I was wasting my life. As soon as I realised what I was doing all that foolish drama and emotion fell away.

When my counselling sessions ended I thought I was on a roll. I quickly found that I slipped back into old habits without noticing it, doing without thinking. That's another story, the point is that you need to keep a careful eye on your Self and another pair of eyes can help in a big way. We seldom see ourselves as other people do.

Buddhist teaching recommends the choice of a teacher or mentor. In practice in our society this is difficult. Finding the right teacher is not easy. From your point of view it is tempting to look for a Guru to make it all better. Someone who can take over you're responsibility and make it easier. This is you slipping back to the Hive all the while convinced that you are on the right Path.

A good teacher will be alert for this, but good teachers are hard to find and always busy. Bad ones are two a penny. Great care is required in the choice of a teacher and great luck or perhaps the intervention of the Universal Power. It is possible to teach your Self, more difficult but possible. After all you have to become sufficiently aware to look for a teacher in the first place. This is done on your own and I suspect most of us will be more or less alone on this journey. However, a good teacher is an excellent aid in maintaining objectivity.

There are ways to help maintain objectivity without a third party. Committing your thoughts to paper helps in the process of removing the wheat from the chaff. In reading and re-reading parts of this book I am both delighted with some of my insights and appalled at others. Hopefully the routine process of checking and editing removes most of the rubbish. It is the disciplined application of the process and the understanding of the need for the process that is important here. It is wise to anticipate and plan for your own mistakes. This is pure Hive strategy, use it for your own ends. Keep a diary of your thoughts, review them routinely at least once a week and edit, edit, edit.

Tune your thoughts in peaceful reflection so that when the time comes you will know and be ready. Reflection, contemplation and meditation are the disciplines which properly direct the actions of sentient beings and dictate how they seek Salvation, how they live their lives.

We set ourselves above other species and pride ourselves on our intellectual powers and yet we rarely do any serious thinking at all. As soon as you stop and think, you will be assailed from all quarters and driven back to action. Stop now and think, allow the chaos to subside and fall away, avoid action for now. Create a relaxed, fearless state of mind, a fertile garden in which you can reclaim your life and give it meaning.

Always give your Self space and time to reflect.

Compassion – for your Self

One of the most important resources available and the most difficult to obtain is compassion for your Self. Not to be confused with self pity, this Self centred approach is not selfish in the negative sense of the word. Your compassion for others will be restricted until you can first feel it for your Self. This recognition of your own pain and vulnerability creates an empathy, a common bond of suffering which allows us to see things differently. For example, if you have personally endured the loss of a loved one then both your ability, and your desire to help others in a similar situation is greatly magnified.

This recognition comes hard since it may be perceived as an admission of weakness. We hide it from those who would exploit it. We hide it from the world and so we hide it from ourselves. The lion looks for the gazelle that limps, therefore do not limp, ignore the pain, hide it away or die. This is what the Hive teaches, but we are not just animals, we are human beings.

Without compassion for your Self, compassion for others all too easily becomes a way of avoiding Self and placating the Hive. The Hive approves of those who work for the Common good expending their lives in selfless good deeds. The suburban jungle is full of such people who feel that they must justify their own purposeless existence through charitable works. Do they feel an empathy with those who they seek to help? Partly perhaps, but their chief motive is often camouflage. They withhold that final sacrifice, that jewel that is Self. Like the miser who hid his gold so well that he could never find it again.

We feel that we are not strong enough or good enough by ourselves. This may have been true in the primordial jungle but we need to evolve past these biological strategies. This is a revolution in evolution, it is the only viable way forward for the individual and therefore the species. We must revolt, the Wheel must turn. We are good enough, we can create our own destiny. We can admit our weakness and take the risk of exposing ourselves. We should not be afraid of failure, only of not trying.

Our own cowardice, fear of disapproval and isolation, drive us unrelentingly away from Self examination and reflection. This Path is a lonely one, give your Self credit for even becoming aware of it. Try to walk it, allow your Self to fail and begin again and again.

Others may help and support you, if you are truly fortunate some may even understand your journey. This is unlikely. Essentially this journey is undertaken with what personal resources you can muster, and with God's Love. By Hive standards this means alone. To progress you will need to believe that you, by your Self, are worthy. This time the needs of the one outweigh those of the many. This is not how we have been trained or even how we feel.

This Self love is so hard for us, on the one hand there is our Hive training, on the other the fear of Self, both powerful inducements to stay with the herd. You have the capacity to become what is your birthright, a unique being beloved of God. Your inevitable mistakes and suffering are only the lessons necessary for your Self development, not reasons for despair or surrender. Don't be frightened of your Self or of getting it wrong.

Remember the small child lying crumpled in the dust, go to her, to your Self, without thought. Put your arms out and kiss away the tears and the pain. Look at the photograph of your Self as a child. God loves you, love your Self, have compassion for your Self.

You need to practice this as you would any new skill. Practice it in your actions towards your Self. For example give your Self time to reflect, set aside any guilt that you may feel. Start the day in peaceful reflection and close the day in the same way. Eat well and sleep well, treat your Self as you would a guest in your home. I don't mean sleep late and stuff your Self, I mean be considerate towards your Self.

Self love

Accept the possibility that God is right to love you, perhaps you are loveable. Then begin to practice loving your Self. Do not try to rationalise it, accept that we all need love. We struggle to give or receive love from any source if we fail to love ourselves. Ask your Self who do you love, who loves you? Is there room for improvement? Of course there is, look at the state of the World we live in. You are not alone, there is little or no real love in our lives. Then begin with your Self. God loves you, now love your Self. Sounds easy? No, you already understand how hard it is or you wouldn't be reading a book like this one.

"You your Self, as much as anybody in the entire Universe, deserve your love and affection."

(Buddha)

Above all, do not dislike, hate or loathe your Self. Do not endlessly criticise and undermine your Self. You do not have to justify your Self to anyone. You cannot be compared for you are incomparable, peerless. Your job is to save your Self, everything else will follow.

Stop measuring your Self and allow your Self the dignity of being, not doing.

Pretend you love your Self to begin with, you cannot suddenly wave a magic wand and make it true. Love is like a seed, first you must prepare the ground, remove the rocks and rubbish, plough the soil and harrow it to create the seed bed. Choose your seed and carefully plant it. Then you water it and watch over it. If you leave it untended the crows will steal it, the weeds will grow up and choke it, the sun will scorch it. Farming is hard work.

If you are going to plant this seed of Self love your actions will speak louder than your words, your life should reflect your beliefs and ideals. Demonstrate your love of your Self through your actions, be a good farmer. You may have to stand over the bare soil and wait for a long time all the while fighting the weeds and wondering if the seed will ever sprout. Eventually it will, the harvest will come.

Use your task orientated Hive skills to master this skill of loving your Self. Be logical and organised.

1. God loves you.
2. You need to love your Self so that you can go to Him.
3. Love your Self so that you can love Him and creation.

Time

Firstly, give your Self the precious gift of time, time to reflect on your inner Self. There are two skills here,

1. Making Time
2. Reflection

Making time for your Self is a difficult task, but it can be learned like any other skill. Salvation is your objective; time management is one of your chief goals. You are not creating time to relax but to reflect and consider your life. Be structured and disciplined, allow your Self precious time. Structure it as best suits you, not your lifestyle.

The lack of time is one of the commonest ways in which we delude ourselves. Like the rabbit in Alice in Wonderland,

"I'm late, I'm late, for a very important date."

By being permanently busy we avoid ourselves, it's like a narcotic and just as difficult a habit to break. Sometimes, sadly the only interruption is death. Be disciplined, your personal time is a priority. I begin everyday with a leisurely cup of tea in bed. For about twenty minutes I allow my Self to wake up in calm reflection, without distraction.

Consider time not like a clock, something you are always up against, but as a generous friend. Try not to think of the small measures of time we plague ourselves with. Think instead of the countless aeons that passed before man, or any living thing, drew a breath. Imagine the Universe forming, millions of galaxies gradually coming together in a time scale beyond our limited comprehension. The next time you are trying to make up five minutes on the way to work at risk of life and limb, think about how ridiculous it is to rush around like a demented hen.

Even in our puny life span we are given seventy or eighty years to play with. Are you really going to spend it leaping out of bed and driving like a maniac? Are you really going to snatch fifteen minutes for a sandwich at lunchtime everyday and come home exhausted too late to see the children before bed?

Before you even try to reorganise your schedule ask your Self why is your life like this. We are addicted to rushing and like any addiction before you can solve the problem you need to examine the root causes not the symptoms. Being frantically busy is acceptable. It is one of the twisted ways in which we measure success,

"Call my secretary and we will try and do lunch next month." Oh Please. Get a grip.

Having time on your hands is for rustic peasants and the unemployed, for losers. That's how we perceive those who take the trouble to make space and time for themselves. How often do we sneer at people who leave work at 4 pm even if they have been in since 8 am? How often do we ask someone,

"What did you do today?"

What we really mean is I did much more than you today because I am important and successful,

"How do you put your time in? Don't you get bored?"

Its not easy believe me. You will face tremendous opposition from your Self in guilt at being seemingly idle and perhaps a sense of unease at the prospect of being alone with your Self. You will also face opposition from those around you. The Hive is intolerant of those who would reflect. Your family may not understand. Do it anyway. Explain if you wish, but do it anyway. Do it even if you do not yet understand why. That will come.

At this point let me re-emphasise how hard this is. Most of you will fail, utterly!

Be unreasonable, allow you're Self to get mad, be determined and stubborn. Just for once you are going to make time for your Self, come what may. Mothers and work aholics take note especially. When guilt leaps up at you recognise it, anticipate it, dump it!

Remember, making time for your Self is a very logical thing to do. A constant lack of time is debilitating, stressful and distracting. Beware, time is the one thing we always deny ourselves. The following chapter on how to assert your Self will be invaluable.

Ironically, too much spare time distresses us. We become agitated, bored, you only have to walk through a shopping mall or DIY store to see how we flee from it. We must fill our time at any cost because it is when we are still with time to reflect that our inner voices are heard. It is when we are alone with our thoughts that we are afraid. Now that we know and understand our objective i.e. personal Salvation, we can muster the courage to be alone with ourselves.

We often label spare time as a boring thing. It is a bit like the addict's early onset of cold turkey. We recognise the signs and become agitated and sweaty. We then begin the frantic search for something to occupy ourselves. Ease your Self in gently, become accustomed to having time before you attempt to use it. Practice doing "nothing". Instead of mowing the lawn talk to your loved ones, its called conversation. Go for an ice cream, read a whole book! Maybe you better start with a magazine with pictures in it, or a newspaper. When you try, you will realise how hard it is. We are programmed to be busy and not to do what we cynically call nothing. Remember you are not doing "nothing", there is no reason to be bored. You are about to enter the lion's den. Ask your Self, are you bored or scared?

If you have trouble identifying with my Hive analogy just watch what happens when you start freeing some time for your Self. The Hive absolutely abhors the thought of you having time to reflect. When you try, it will suddenly step out of the shadows and become apparent. Have some fun with it. Try it on the wife when she wants you to mow the lawn or your husband when he wants his dinner. Just say,

"I'm thinking, you'll have to wait."

Tell your boss that you need some time everyday to just sit and think. Even better try it on your co-workers and friends.

Anger is not generally a useful thing, it can be in this instance. When the Hive pressures you into doing and prevents you from having time to reflect, allow your Self to get a little mad. Why after all these years should you not have a little time to sort your Self out? Just for once do something for your Self without guilt or fear.

Remember that the Hive is also in you. You will be afraid to do these things, even just trying will put you in a sweat. You must come to terms with the process before you even think about trying it on other people. Your Hive conditioning has to be broken or at least challenged before you can advance. This is very, very difficult, don't be too hard on your Self.

Without objectives or direction we are right to be afraid, remember you are not creating time to do nothing or relax, far from it. You are creating a precious space in which to work towards your own Salvation. You absolutely must have time to do this from a practical point of view. It is also imperative that you begin to free your Self mentally from the influence of the Hive. You must separate your Higher and lower self so that your Higher Self can take charge of your life.

We work best if our time is scheduled, structured, an act of discipline. Build it into your daily regime, use the traits that you have learned from the Hive. The work ethic, structure, logic use them all. Prepare the ubiquitous action plan, chapter 15, become your own centre of excellence. These can be effective tools, use them. If your objective is clear they will comfort you like familiar faces. It is impossible and devastating to try and rip your Self from every aspect of the Hive's illusion so carefully created over the years.

Initially you will be able to do little Self reflection with the time you make. You will be too busy fighting to get it and becoming familiar with the concept. It will seem like Self indulgence, wrong, alien. Give your Self time, adjust to having time. Becoming accustomed to having time for your Self will take a surprising amount of effort. We are so used to doing that we ignore being. The new you is different, tell your Self,

"I don't just do, I am."

To use the conflict analogy again you cannot suddenly pick up the skills required to use such a sophisticated weapon as time overnight. Drawing the blade does not make you a swordsman. Before you can use it effectively you must master it. Having time is a state of mind.

It is only when you are comfortable with it and have the confidence to fend of the criticism that will come your way that its true value will become apparent. It took me about a year before I became even slightly comfortable with the idea, it's a big thing, it will not happen overnight. At this point you will guard your Self and your time as a Tigress defends her cubs. All your time, your whole life, infinity, will be recaptured and given meaning.

Everyday, every hour, your search for fulfilment will be in your thoughts and it will be the most natural thing in the world. It will not be difficult, it will be your natural state, an elevated form of consciousness. This is where you are supposed to be. You will be calmer, easier to live with and vastly more productive and creative. You will literally become a powerhouse for positive innovation. You will think objectively, logically and strategically. You will be senior management material, infinitely better able to manage your own life let alone some piddly company.

In chapter 15, the action plan, you will find time management as one of your primary goals. This is a long term project and will require dogged determination and Self discipline. I would expect to see it as a primary goal for several years before it becomes almost second nature. Even then it requires constant practice and vigilance to prevent you from regressing. There are some useful resources to help you in your studies at the end of this chapter and in appendix 1.

Remember much of this stuff is work related, designed to create more efficient drones. You are more interested in creating time for your Self, not in improving your productivity. You are using the Hive's tactics against it. Do not get sucked into doing, concentrate on being.

Structure and Discipline

Once again, forewarned is forearmed, you will go astray from time to time. Learn from my experience and plan for this contingency. How? Well by using those old Hive favourites, structure and discipline. These two stalwarts can help you avoid going astray and help you pick it up when it happens. Time will be the main problem, but we have already covered that one, haven't we? Create structured space in your daily routine, for example.

Eden's Legacy

> 6.00 A.M. Wake and make tea, back to bed for twenty minutes quiet reflection.
> Meditation/prayer/contemplation.
> Bathroom/breakfast.
> Travel to work.

On your journey to work remember to treat others as you would wish to be treated. Depending on how you travel stay calm and do not undo the good work you have already done that morning. On arrival at work concentrate fully on the tasks at hand. Try to take a short mid morning break and a decent nutritious lunch away from your place of work. If there is time go for a walk or read.

> Noon, lunch.
> 1 P.M. Back to work, again try for a mid afternoon break if you can.
> 5 P.M. Leave work, tomorrow is a new day.

On the journey home keep calm and be considerate. As a rule you should not take work home. If you can't get it done during the proper time you need to take steps to sort out the problem. Do not let your work become an excuse.

> Physical exercise, gym, Judo, run, bike, swim.
> Dinner/family. Relax watch TV, socialise.

Reflect on your day, plan your meditation for the following morning. A good nights sleep is essential. Without adequate sleep you will spiral out of control.
    I can hear you laughing from here. Life is not like that I hear you say, the wife, the kids, work. This guy has never had kids, he doesn't understand the pressure I'm under. Fine, stop being negative and produce your own schedule. Everybody is different, time management is an industry, read and learn about it. Don't squabble over the details, look at the bigger picture. It's your life, take charge of it. It is all too easy to read an interesting book and forget about it. This is about your whole life, not just another book. It's a power struggle and you must win. Draw up a schedule that you can aspire to, build it up gradually.

The key point here is that you would rather scoff at my schedule and talk about my naivety than tackle it your Self. The schedule is merely a tool, before it can be effective you have to realise the mess your in. You need to discern the conflict and engage your Self in it willingly.

To do that you must control the things that will directly effect your ability to evolve. Stop letting things happen and start making them happen.

Create a positive constructive and calm environment in which you can you use your God given intelligence to solve the dilemma of your own life.

Meditation

Having the time leads naturally to reflection, there is a great danger here that you will be overwhelmed by all of this. In this quest you are always a heartbeat from disaster. Depression, frustration, isolation, confusion and despair, every deadly, poisonous dart that the Hive can throw. To attempt the journey alone is beyond the powers of most of us. Fortunately we are not alone.

Your fellow travellers past and present have left a trail for you to follow. They have learned, as we all must learn, that there is a place on the Path where we can only proceed by helping others. The paradox of the selfish search for Self and our mutual interdependence becomes clear. All that they have learned and experienced is available to you through literature, television and the Internet.

To help you master the weapon of time and the art of reflection I would strongly advise the study of meditation. It will help to control your inevitable fear and anxiety at having time available for the frightening task ahead of you. It will keep you calm and clear headed and allow you to mix with like minded people who can support you. Meditation is distinct and separate from religion.

The subject of meditation has been extensively written about by those better qualified than I, study it, practice it. It will save you much pain and confusion. Remember it is a tool to help you realise your own dream of Salvation. This is a powerful, potentially life altering discipline, treat it with healthy respect and recognise your dependence on the teachings of others. You will find more information in appendix 1, at the end of this chapter you will find one exercise, the Meditation on the Bodies which I particularly enjoy.

A word of warning, meditation has become very fashionable, as has Buddhism. Many people have become enmeshed in the religion at the expense of their Spirituality, it is a very fine line. Remember your Spiritual independence and your sole responsibility for Self. Before you shave your head and don the robes check your motives. Do not allow your Self do be distracted by the romance of an exotic dalliance with the mystic East. It is a means to an end, not an end in itself.

This is not a denigration of Buddhism, from which I have learned a great deal. Rather it is a warning of our own tendency to be sucked in by the Hive and distracted when we think we are making the most progress.

Meditation is a means of controlling the process of reflection. We are at our best with structure, discipline and logic, use these Hive tools to control the pace of your journey, it will prevent many a crash. Explore it for your Self. I find it especially helpful in understanding my emotions, particularly those emotions that are rooted in the subconscious. For example we often get angry when we are scared. Our anger seems powerful, consuming but really we are just afraid. (See chapter 14). Emotions are usually symptomatic of some deeper conflict, a little time spent in meditation helps to uncover the root causes of these problems.

Meditation is a way of amplifying the still small voice that sometimes struggles to be heard, it can help in dissipating the illusions with which we surround ourselves. We have within us all the tools we need to find Peace. Meditation can help us to create the correct setting for the Truth to emerge. The act of learning about meditation can provide stimulation and relief from isolation. Learn with others, share your insights and experiences, carefully.

"It is crucial for you to understand what meditation is. It is not some special posture, and it's not just a set of mental exercises. Meditation is the cultivation of mindfulness and the application of that mindfulness once cultivated. You do not have to sit to meditate. You can meditate while washing the dishes. You can meditate in the shower, or roller skating, or typing letters. Meditation is awareness, and it must be applied to each and every activity of one's life. This isn't easy."

Henepola Gunaratana, (Mindfulness in Plain English)

Meditation is a powerful defence and a potent weapon in your war with the Hive. It is a life skill that should stay with you for the rest of your days. Practice it diligently even if initially it does not seem to be for you. Persevere with it and it will pay huge dividends. Here are some useful resources for your studies.

Books
How to meditate, by John Novak.
Meditation for dummies, by Stephen Bodian.
The stages of meditation, by the Dalai Lama.
Concentration and Meditation by Christmas Humphries.
The idiots guide to meditation, by Jeff Davidson.

Websites
www.meditationcentre.com
www.kadampa.com
www.wildmind.com

The Meditation on the Bodies

I am not my body, I am not my emotions, I am not my thoughts.

The purpose of this meditation is to disentangle Self from the several vehicles of our consciousness that comprise our earthly existence. It also allows us to become familiar with the concept of a detached Self which gradually merges with the Universal Consciousness.

The more adept you become the greater the feeling of detachment and peace and the further that you will travel. Begin with short trips and build up gradually. Be cautious, there are no limits to how far you can go, but it takes time. As you become comfortable and more relaxed with the exercise you will find that you feel more centred and calm, all things will be in perspective, in their proper place.

Eden's Legacy

Begin by sorting out a quiet place where you will not be disturbed at all. Make your Self comfortable so that you will not be distracted by cramp or stiffness. You may be engrossed in the exercise for some time. Sit in the classic position on the floor or in a chair, or against a wall, just so long as you are comfortable. Your back should be straight if possible.

Technically you should start learning about concentration before you attempt more basic exercises in meditation than this one. However I can't resist telling you about this one. I will assume that you are going to enrol in a class and this is a sample of what is to come.

Breath deeply and evenly, for the moment concentrate on this alone. Clear your mind and relax breathing slowly in and out. When your breathing is deep and slow begin to examine your body for sensation. Start with your feet, are they warm, cold, can you feel anything? Move up your legs to your hips and back doing the same thing, looking for sensation. Breathing long and slow. Check your neck and shoulders, your arms and hands and your head. Imagine it is somebody else's body, what can you feel?

Say to your Self,
"This is my body, not me, I am not my body."

Feel sensations and ignore them, for the moment they belong only to your body. Imagine your body where it is now. Watch your body as you would somebody else. Pull back from your body and look at it from the four corners of the room. Walk around your body. Come up close to it and examine its features carefully. There is your body beside your Self.

Now, still breathing slow and deep, what emotions are you aware of in your Self at the moment? Go through all the emotions and look for them as you did with your body. Anger, fear, jealousy, hate, love, envy, contempt, shame, happiness, pity. Pick one that particularly applies to you at the moment. Feel it, examine it, why is it? Take fear for example. This time imagine your Self above your body looking down. Search for signs of emotion. Say to your Self,

"this person is afraid of the past," or whatever the fear is based on.
Then say to your Self,
"I am not afraid, I am not my body, I am not my emotions. I am not afraid."

Feel your Self floating higher and higher without feeling or emotion. Look down and see a person meditating quietly in a room. Look down and see a house in which a person meditates. Look down and see a town far below. Drawing further away all the time, now you can see a continent from Earth's orbit, now you can see Earth.

Still breathing deep and slow consider your thoughts as they float through your mind. You have been thinking about your body and about your emotions and what is happening to you. Let your thoughts float across your minds eye like clouds in the sky. Don't try and hold them or examine them, let them drift through your mind, try and clear your mind of all thoughts. As thoughts come into your mind watch them drift across, let them go, do not try to force them out or hold them back. Say to your self,

"I am not my body, I am not my emotions, I am not my thoughts."

Recognise the difference between thinking about something and understanding or knowing a thing. Thinking about something, for example your aches and pains, is a product of your lower mind. Understanding or knowing a thing, for example the difference between right and wrong, is a product of your higher mind. Follow your higher mind, where does this knowledge come from?

It is your higher mind that is connected to the Universal Consciousness. Draw further back until you can see the Sun and the Moon beside the Earth, further back until you can see the whole Milky Way. Further and further, more galaxies appear, hundreds and thousands of galaxies. Slowly they become fewer, further between, there is more darkness. Further again, right up to the edge of the dark void and further, to what?

As you follow it at some point, in the future, you will come to a place that you do not know. A place that is beyond your experience or comprehension without limits or restrictions. Here the Self merges with the Universal Consciousness and becomes one, unfettered by restraints of time or physical being. The Meditation On The Bodies is designed to bring you to this place. From here you can understand reality and examine your chosen subject, gaining knowledge and Enlightenment.

Finally when you can go no further, enjoy being. Later you will be using this place as a study in which to meditate on your chosen subject. For now just enjoy the sensation, the thrill of the connection. To return, imagine a sky diver plummeting through space towards Earth. Through the galaxies, through the planets, through the clouds towards a continent, a town, a house. As the house where the person meditates appears, pull your parachute and float gently down to land beside that person. As you walk towards them you can see the peaceful expression on their face. Stretch out your hand and touch them on the shoulder, gently.

To conclude, stay very still, breathing slow and deep for a few minutes to regain your balance. Sometimes I enjoy the journey so much I am reluctant to return. At other times I am unable to go far at all. It is important to persevere and to practice. Ideally you will be learning under the supervision of a teacher as part of a class. This exercise is a sample of things to come.

Material Resources

Treat your search for personal fulfilment as you would a college course. Use all the facilities and resources you can think of.

The Human Archive.

The written word is a powerful teacher, but what we are really talking about is the transfer of information. For thousands of years this has largely been done through story telling, memory and the written word. Of course this will continue but this uniquely human capacity has been augmented by other mediums. Our ability to influence and teach others has developed with the advent of television and more recently the Internet.

This is potentially a good thing. How we use this information has always been a reflection of the age old conflict between Good and Evil. That has not changed, but for the discerning Seeker more priceless information than ever before is freely and easily available.

Television

Times change, the need to communicate wisdom and ideas does not. There is a lot of intellectual snobbery around literature that puts a lot of people off reading anything serious. There are however a lot of clever, wise people who are able to communicate their message in the glittering format of the silver screen. For some f my choices see appendix 2. Much of what we watch is pure rubbish, some of it downright dangerous.

What children watch especially is a matter of grave concern. Do not assume the cartoons your children watch in the mornings are harmless. Supervise their TV viewing carefully. Each program is screened with its own rating, use the parental control facilities on most modern television's and lock out those programs not appropriate for your children. The censors go to a lot of trouble to screen programs and this is important, but it is your responsibility as a parent to supervise.

Even if you pay little heed to what your children watch there are those who give it the most careful consideration, for all kinds of reasons!

Take more of an interest in your viewing, regulate it, consider how much time you spend watching TV and why. If it is not educational or serving a positive end why watch it? TV tends to hog our attention because it is so easy, too easy. It can be recreational and this is perfectly legitimate but be cautious, this is too powerful and dynamic a medium for Good or Evil to be taken lightly. Use it as a tool for education and Enlightenment, not to kill time or sedate the children.

As a medium for education and for influencing people, especially the young, it is unsurpassed. Wisdom is where you find it. Some of my choices are in appendix 2. Take the time to watch these movies, what could be easier in today's lifestyle? Nip out to the video store and augment your reading. Reinforce the message with the movie. At the end of each chapter you will see a resources section which will often include some recommended viewing. Incorporate these films and documentaries into your recreation, look for others that might inspire or provide insight. Add to the list, talk to people on the net, compare and discuss. Enjoy them but at the same time consider the messages contained within them, be aware of the attempt at communication with you as a sentient being.

The Internet

This book will be available on the Internet, if I have the skills or access to them, I can reach millions instead of a few thousand as an ordinary book would. It can also be interactive, people can reach me, set up chat rooms, email each other. It is relatively cheap, accessible to a much greater audience and the permutations are limitless. Everybody can have an input.

Eden's Legacy

The Internet is also a defence against the isolation that the Seeker will face. The human archive is full of the teachings of other Spiritual Warriors. The story of their journeys are set out for those wise enough to seek them. I am constantly astonished when I perform an on line search for something I consider obscure and esoteric only to find hundreds of references. All of them connected to individuals to whom I can communicate. This matrix is not limited by geography or language, it is a huge step forward in the struggle toward the light. Use it.

It is said that there is nothing new under the sun. Whatever you are undergoing has been endured before. Not in exact detail for you are unique. The point is that you can learn from what others have experienced. This ability is a pivotal strength of any civilised society, sadly it is greatly neglected. As a society we are cohesive and organised in our own time but we still have not mastered the science and art of History. We are preoccupied with now and often fail to learn from then. Many of us, not having the wit to seek knowledge, must wait for the heart attack or the car crash before we are motivated to examine our lives.

As you study you will discover with some surprise that you are not alone. This sharing of knowledge is a great source of wisdom and comfort. Some of the most inspirational relationships you will form will be with fellow Spiritual Warriors long dead.

Their thought and words are as powerful today as they were when the authors were alive. A life's work can and does shake off the heavy yoke of mortality through the written word. Thousands and thousands of good people have written down the hard won wisdom of their experience for the sake of today's generation and those yet unborn.

The great sadness is that this knowledge lies untapped, but it is there! Fantastic, earth shattering, life altering wisdom hidden on the dusty shelves of your local library. The lack is not in availability it is in the desire for wisdom. The desire for wisdom comes with awareness and awareness comes when? It is a gradual process driven primarily by suffering although it can come to a head quickly, even suddenly.

As a sentient you are Self aware and can define the nature of your own destiny. To what extent is a mystery, but no other species on this planet has the ability to promote itself to an Enlightened state of awareness in this fashion. We can make the leap within our own lifetime, what happens thereafter is a matter of personal belief. You have the choice.

Awareness brings responsibility and change, the harbingers of fear. You have to want to find it. Most people are ignorant of it or seek to avoid it. You no longer fit into either category. It is time to begin the search for Self, it is time for the next level.

This stealing of time and learning to reflect and study are the first acts of mutiny against the tyranny of the Hive. Prepare for the counter attack!

The primary threat will undoubtedly come from within. The secondary attack will be from those around you. The following powerful threats and corresponding counter measures will be discussed in the next chapters.

Your own Self doubt.
Guilt.
Your desire to belong and to be accepted.
Your desire for material wealth.
Isolation.
Weariness from over exposure and the need for balance.

The secondary attack will come from those around you. Your work mates, friends and acquaintances, family, even strangers. In the following chapters we will learn to recognise all these enemies and how to combat them.

Resources, see also appendix 1 and 2.

Books - How to get control of your time and your life, by Dan Lakein. Time tactics of very successful people, by B. Eugene Griessman. The time trap, by R. Alec MacKenzie.
Movies - Clockwise with John Cleese.
Websites - www.timemanagementguide.com, www.worldwidelearn.com

Chapter 10, Asserting your Self

Assertion Skills – Useful for both Offence and Defence of Self.

What is assertion? To assert your Self requires Self awareness and Self respect. It also requires a sympathetic awareness and respect for other people and their needs. You need to understand your own needs and be able communicate them openly and honestly without hurting anyone else.

By asserting your Self you are accepting that you and you alone are responsible for your Self. This is the behaviour of a strong, wise and mature person. It also goes against much of what we have been taught about social interaction and how to get what we want.

The Hive prefers conflict and competition, this is how we commonly get what we want as illustrated below in the four basic types of non assertive behaviour. Assertive behaviour requires that the individual is calm and centred and non threatening. Most of us expect to have to fight for what we want and confuse aggression with assertion. We win or we lose, we succeed or we fail. Conflict.

We do not have a clear idea of what our personal needs are, we concentrate too much on specific instances or situations that we like or dislike. For example after a long hard day at work Fred comes home late and finds the house is a mess, the kids are being noisy and there is no sign of dinner. He bangs about, grumpily throwing things in the sink annoying his wife Wilma who has had the kids all day and is just about ready for a break. A moody husband is not what she needs. Two opposing factions, both tired and both feeling a little Self righteous. The inevitable row solves nothing, it polarises the two sides and makes both Fred and Wilma feel bad.

Fred has a right to some peace and quiet but it is up to Fred to express his need and organise its fulfilment. He does not have the right to expect his wife to hug him on the doorstep and put his dinner on the table. The trouble is that is what he usually gets, what he is used to. So when it doesn't happen, he becomes grumpy.

Gabriel Deeds

Wilma also has a right to some peace and quiet but it is up to her to convey her needs to Fred in a consistent manner so that he knows what is expected. It is no good attacking Fred only when she is particularly tired and letting him get away with it on other occasions. She is responsible for organising her own peace and quiet. Neither is telepathic or stupid although we could be forgiven for thinking they were both.

Fred would like his ego massaged after a hard day at work. Is that a need, no, it is a vague desire and he does not consider his wife at all. He demonstrates no respect for his wife or her demanding role in running the home. If he was to consider his need carefully he might realise that he is feeling insecure after a hard day at the Hive and wants to re establish his role as the dominant male and bread winner. He wants to feel good about himself but at Wilma's expense. He might need to look into that.

If he was to say to Wilma,
"Sorry I'm late dear, I didn't mean to leave you so long with the kids. I had a problem at work, give me a hug and I will bath the children." Things might have been different. Wilma on the other hand might decide that she is going to accept the traditional role of a housewife and butter old Fred up a bit. His dinner will be on the table and she will support his need to be stroked. The thing is it's a two way street and he will have to trade.

Good, honest and open communication is the key. We are very poor at communicating how we feel. To disclose your feelings is a risky thing to do. How can anyone take account of your feelings if they are unaware of them? Lets face it men and women are very different. What seems obvious to one person may be completely overlooked by another. Especially if they are of different gender. Try communicating your feelings, not just to your partner but to a wider circle of the people who surround you. You will be surprised at the results.

We fail to understand our own needs and suppress them so that by the time we express them we have lost our composure and come across as aggressive. In the following you will find a list of everyone's basic personal rights and some pointers on how to make sure you get them. A little time considering your needs and especially those of your nearest and dearest will pay big dividends.

It is ironic but the more you give to others the more you receive. If you think less of your own problems and needs and more about those of the people around you, you will be surprised at the results. Look on it as another way to get what you need.

If you want to be able to make time for the study of your Self it would be wise to brush up on your assertion skills. Once again I do not intend to go into the subject in depth. You will find a list of recommended reading on the subject in appendix 1 and at the end of this chapter. Like any skill, if you are serious about improving your lot you will need to invest some time and effort in mastering it. Although it takes a little practice, results can be surprisingly swift.

There are four basic behaviour types associated with people who have problems asserting themselves. We are all guilty and we do not necessarily stick to the same kind of non assertive behaviour all the time but we each have our favourites. Which is your speciality?

Submissive behaviour,

Putting your Self second and appeasing others. You do not behave as if you are important and fail to communicate your needs to others. You feel that rather than impose your wishes on others you would rather take a back seat and let them figure out your needs. When they fail to or get it wrong you get upset and they get confused.

Aggressive behaviour,

Aggressive people do not care about anyone else, they only care about getting what they want. They will use physical force, coercion, intimidation, whatever it takes. They alienate everybody, but then, they don't care.

Passive-aggressive behaviour,

This type of behaviour is a kind of overlapping of the first two. Being indirectly aggressive involves bad behaviour designed to indirectly communicate subconscious or conscious needs. Passive-aggressive people seldom get what they want because they do not really know what they want themselves and do not communicate honestly and directly. Other people are frustrated and angered by this type of behaviour.

Manipulative behaviour

   Instead of communicating openly and honestly manipulative people make other people feel sorry or guilty towards them. To get what they want rather than what they need, they play the victim or martyr rather than take responsibility for themselves. It only works short term because sooner or later those subjected to such behaviour get wise to it and become resentful.

Assertive Behaviour

   To assert your Self requires Self awareness and Self respect. It also requires a sympathetic awareness and respect for other people and their needs. You need to understand your own needs and be able communicate them openly and honestly without hurting anyone else.

   Needs and rights, rights and needs. There is no clear defining barrier between the two. Here is a list of personal rights to help you explore the concept. Put them up on the fridge door.

Personal Rights

I have the right to time and space.

I have the right to study my Self.

I have the right to consider and express my needs.

I have the right to help and support from other people.

I have the right to say No.

I have the right to be fallible, i.e. wrong, afraid, emotional.

I have the right to be treated with honesty, dignity and respect.

I have the right to make my own decisions.

I have the right to change my mind.

I am not responsible for other people's problems.

Gabriel Deeds

How to be Assertive.

As always begin with your Self. Before you can be assertive you must have respect and understanding of your own rights. Then you must realise that others have the same rights. Of course this means that you will not always get your own way, but you may be surprised at how often you do. When you show respect for other people's dignity and sympathy for their situation it is surprising how obliging they can be.

This is a new way of solving your problems, not the way you have been taught. Unfortunately we are not taught how to assert ourselves whilst we are young. Perhaps someday it will be on the curriculum of every school, in the meantime we must learn the skill as adults. You cannot simply read this text and become assertive. You must practice and study if you are to master the business of asserting your Self.

Your basic rights above are also the basic rights of everyone else. You cannot assert your Self in conflict at someone else's expense, that is mere aggression. This is the way we have been taught, the problem is that this way there is always a loser. Furthermore, by winning in this fashion at the expense of another, you do not really win at all. Both parties are injured.

To begin with assert your Self consciously, and deliberately. After practice and becoming more experienced you will learn to be assertive spontaneously. Begin by selecting a situation that is a problem for you. Carefully write up a description of your problem. Reflect on,

What you are feeling?
What it is you want to achieve?
What are your personal rights?
What are the rights of the other party?

Be very specific with the who, what, why, when, where and who. Do not be vague.

You should also try to put your Self in the other persons position, try to anticipate their feelings and needs before promoting your own. Here is an example.

I seem to be the only one around here who does any house work. No matter how hard a day I have had at work I am expected to do most of the cooking and cleaning and look after the kids. I am sick of ranting and raving about it and nobody paying any attention. I go mad and things improve for a few days and then go back to normal.

Not an unusual situation these days. Lets tighten things up a bit.

Who do you have the problem with? - My husband and family.
When does it occur? – All the time.
How does it make you feel? – Angry, undervalued, demeaned.
What do you need?

What do you need is not so easy a question as you might think. The answer could simply be a maid or a bit more help from the husband. Why does she feel demeaned and undervalued? There is a lack of recognition of the individual's dignity and respect. Being taken for granted is a very hurtful thing, it might even be construed as aggressive behaviour, a form of violence.

Or it could be that Mum sees herself as the skivvy and lets them get away with it, perhaps her Self esteem is so low, perhaps she is unaware or uncaring of her rights and her responsibility to her Self. She does not assert her Self and so others discount her.

Ask again, what does she need? Things are seldom what they seem, especially people. She needs to be loved and appreciated by her family, however until she loves and respects her Self and consistently asserts her rights they will take her for granted. It is easy to run for cover when the wife blows her top, just pop down to the pub until she calms down, even joke about it with the boys. This is a far more serious problem than it might appear to be. So how do we approach it? Be very specific about,
    1.   What you are feeling.
    2.   What you want to happen.

An angry housewife may just be the tip of the iceberg. When you are clear about these two points, sit down with your partner and arrange a time and place to discuss the problem. Remember to carefully consider your rights and those of your partner.

It is your responsibility to communicate clearly the problem as you see it and their consequences. Express your feelings, they are real.

Gabriel Deeds

Remember although clear to you they may be a shock to your partner. We are not good at communicating or reading minds.

Ask for what you want, no demands or ultimatums and absolutely do not criticise.

Do not threaten, coerce, cajole or apologise, keep your request clear and simple. Concentrate on how their behaviour makes you feel. Even if they deny the action they cannot deny how you feel. If necessary write down the whole thing including the anticipated responses of the other party.

The other party may have valid points to make and feelings that you have not considered. You are not taking up an entrenched position in a conflict, it may be necessary to make adjustments, to compromise in the details. Decide where and when you will draw the line and what will happen if you do not agree. Do not be afraid of taking time to think about it overnight for example, you are not at war.

For example Fred might say that he feels that he does his share outside in the garden. He might genuinely believe that and it may be necessary to persuade him otherwise or you might offer to help him cut the hedges if he helps out around the house. Negotiate do not demand. By being prepared to assert your Self you may encourage others to do the same. This is a good thing.

Be careful at this stage to prevent a descent into conflict. If you feel that you are getting angry, say so and why. Calm, resolute requests will have more effect than shouting. If necessary break off before things go to far. Sometimes when people are surprised in these situations they can react unpredictably, try to anticipate. Most people handled in this assertive manner will react favourably to your requests.

Saying No

The thoughtless word causes more strife in this life than we can know. Especially that small but deadly word, yes. It seems to slip out when we least expect it to and when often, given time to reflect, we would make our excuses or simply say, no. We are basically endowed with the desire to help if we can. It may be as a result of our social upbringing and the way that all primates cooperate together, a desire to please, or it could be natural goodness. It certainly does not afflict everyone for we do not all possess a giving nature. Many of us have hardened our hearts as a result of experience, cynicism or selfishness.

To those of us loosely labelled as "givers", the type of person who I hope will be reading this book, the word "yes" is a constant problem. Especially now that you have realised that you have the right and indeed a responsibility, to your Self. You will get absolutely nowhere in your search for Self until you recognise your need and absolute right to say, "No."

Far from being a good, kind thing, saying yes at your own expense is dangerous, debilitating and distracting. Telling your Self that it is right is merely weakness, a waste of your Self no matter how good the deed. For now you know that, you, come first and then, them. Sometimes it is easier to give in and say yes, to do what is required and put Self aside. That must change if you are to proceed.

A lack of time and thought are often the only problem. Remember to give your Self, as much time as you need, don't ration it. Cultivate the inner calm and space to reflect that we all need. Hesitate before opening your mouth, think before you speak, weigh your words carefully. The slightest of moments is often all that is required. Let us imagine a spontaneous situation in which you are suddenly asked to dinner by the boss on the one night you have set aside for a hot bath and a book. Your initial reaction to the request, very often the most honest, is horror. He has just asked you and waits expectantly for your reply.

Firstly there would seem to be no time, if you are unable to take some, make some.

Taking time

"Thank you for the tempting offer but I already have plans for that evening." No excuses.

Making time

"That would be lovely, but I better check with my partner first, I think she had something planned. I will call you tomorrow."

Someday you will be Self assured enough to take time and assert your Self easily and naturally, but for now we are probably looking at making time. We can admit that we are fallible and build up to it gradually. Even the most assertive amongst us get caught out from time to time. When you feel pressured or flustered you need time. Time to recover your composure and time to reflect. Do not compromise on this one. Even if you feel a fool or feel embarrassed, give your Self time.

Next, consider why you would be tempted to say yes even though you don't want to.

> It is easier to say yes.
> You would rather say yes than risk giving offence.
> You put the needs of others before your own needs.
> You see your Self as less important than others.
> There may be a benefit to your Self in saying yes.
> The boss doesn't do this very often and he's a bit nervous about it.

It may be that enduring an evening with your boss would benefit your career. It might be that you decide to support him at a difficult time. Reflect and make your decision. If however there is no specific benefit or reason it would be wrong to say yes.

In saying no there are certain rules depending on the situation. Always be firm and polite, look them right in the eye and smile. For a stranger trying to sell you something a straight forward,

"No, thank you," will suffice. If necessary repeat your Self using a slightly more forceful tone, keeping your posture upright and open. Do not look down or away, don't fold your arms. For a friend you may feel it necessary to explain or even go a step further and offer an alternative.

"Not tonight, I'm really tired, I just need to crash. How about another night in the week?" Offer an alternative, if you want to, not out of guilt.

We can say, "yes", in our actions not just in our words. If you do all the cooking and cleaning automatically in your house you are saying,

"Yes, this is my job."

The same possible reasons as above apply but by doing it without question you have said yes to the task. Women tend to fall victim to this type of non assertion because they feel that it is their job. That may be the case but these days all to often they are also working outside the home and it is unfair to expect them to do all the chores. Women also tend to be more nurturing in their outlook falling prey to their giving tendencies.

To assert your Self in this situation requires discipline and consistency. To say "no" in this situation means not doing the job just because someone else doesn't want to or doesn't do it as well as you would like. If you do it most of the time and only occasionally blow your top you are guilty of sending mixed messages.

If you are saying "yes" by doing and getting angry and bitter about it you are harming your Self, belittling your Self and confusing those around you. Evaluate your rights and needs, assemble the family, simply state the problem and how you feel and make your requests. Perhaps a fair division of labour or a rota or a total delegation. It is the process that is important. Then you must prevent your Self from going back to your old ways of doing rather than thinking. Give your Self priority.

If you hold your Self in high esteem and are aware of your value and worth then you will find it easier to assert your Self. By practicing the skill of Self assertion you will come to appreciate your Self more and so increase your Self esteem. Yet another cycle that you must be "aware" of if you are to develop.

Resources, see also appendix 1 and 2.

Books - Men are From Mars Women Are From Venus, Asserting yourself by Sharon and Gordon Bower.
Movies – Educating Rita.

Chapter 11   Self Defence

As soon as you begin your search for Self you will be attacked and undermined. The attack will come from within your Self and from those around you. Sometimes it will be subtle, sometimes gross. It will be cumulative and remorseless! Remember, this conflict is for possession of your true Self, your soul. The stakes could not be higher. Remember also that by trying to take control of your life you have declared war.

All this sounds terrible but remember the state you are in now. This is no worse than you now endure as a slave. Now however you are going to recapture your whole existence from the Hive. The following chapters are intended to help you understand what will happen to you and to prepare for it. You will need help, this is going to be tough.

You will not suddenly find peace happiness and fulfilment, this is another delusion. You are assuming the burden of responsibility for your Self. We prefer to suffer with the familiar devils we know than strive for improvement. The difference is that your suffering will be your teacher, it will serve a purpose, you will have a mission. You will also be a much wiser stronger person with powerful allies. The rewards far outweigh the penalties.

Human kind can endure almost unlimited suffering, we know this from bitter experience. Give us an objective and a common foe and just watch what we can do, suffering is almost irrelevant. We just shrug it off and go on, call it blitz mentality. Take away our objectives and goals, make the enemy invisible, isolate us from our neighbours and you will see true misery such as we now endure.

The enemy, what enemy? The Hive is hard to spot, it is insidious, like the modern terrorist it does not field an army that can be destroyed. It is like organised crime, reaching into our society, pervading all and yet intangible. It seems as though the Hive is the natural order of things, what can one person do? It seems that all you can do is keep your head down and avoid trouble, if you can bear it!

The fly in the ointment is our own still small voice, relentlessly asking the one question we flinch from. Why? Why am I here? Without an adequate answer to this devastatingly simple question we cannot abide our own lives. We are caught between two opposing factions,

Eden's Legacy

Good and Evil. Paralysed by fear and ignorance we cannot access the arsenal of weapons that we have within us. Sooner or later we have to begin the process of recovering our lives. Our mission, to save ourselves and help others to do the same.

In the hope that you have decided to continue here are some tips on what to expect and how to protect your Self.

If you are interested in finding out more about your Self it will probably be as a result of dissatisfaction with your current state of affairs. Or you have reached a point in your life where you need to know and understand rather than just accept. Now is your time! Yes it is a difficult task but the pointless suffering you have thus far endured has made you restless and bold.

The Threshold of Knowing

We all have the desire for happiness and fulfilment. When these things are absent as they so often are in modern living we begin to question. Mark this place in your life, before you go any further. You have reached the threshold of a new dimension, the Threshold of Knowing. I say mark it because you will come running back with your tail between your legs, everybody does. This is quite normal, do not be despondent when it happens. It means that you are finally fighting the right fight.

You will need to find this place again, you will need to remember why you began the journey in the first place. When you are driven back by Self doubt, guilt, confusion and fear, rally your resources. Keep this book handy, you will need to read it, often. It was here you realised how unhappy you were and decided to do something about it. Remember the things that you disliked about your life.

Gabriel Deeds

Here are some of the things that I disliked about my life.

1. It lacked meaning, I had no objective, no reason to be.
2. I had no time, I was always too busy.
3. I was becoming cynical and bitter, not a nice person.
4. I was becoming more manipulative and devious at work.
5. I had no real friends only acquaintances. (Be honest)
6. The job, the house, the car, I was always worried about money, my debts were increasing.
7. I was depressed, unhappy, always angry.
8. I could not bear to be alone with myself, had to be busy.
9. My family became the butt of my frustration, I felt trapped.
10. I was drinking too much and taking sleeping pills.
11. I was in poor physical condition, off sick a lot and putting on weight. I always had a headache.
12. My work and relationships began to suffer.

<u>Please</u> take a few minutes and make your own list for your action plan, it is important that you do it now!

All of these and more, commonly afflict modern humanity, especially in the affluent West. You will no doubt recognise some old acquaintances on the list. They are all symptomatic of conflict, war in fact. The brutal, relentless war between your lower Self, desire, emotion, intellect and your Higher Spiritual Self an unknown entity. As your Spiritual Self evolves and makes itself felt even unconsciously the conflict grows. The war is for control of the whole Self, Darkness verses the Light.

The mid life crisis is a classic example. After forty odd years of living the life of a drone without purpose we naturally rebel. After forty years our subconscious sentience has grown strong enough and we are wiser in the ways of the world, less biddable than we once were. We dare to openly challenge the authority of the Hive.

This is a good thing, even if we feel confused and depressed, it is a sign of hope. Many or even most people do not perceive the struggle, they merely endure it or are so immersed in satisfying their lower self's needs they do not see.

"Life's a bitch, and then you die" They are slaves, dumb bovine drones who must wait for their own evolution. Do not despise them however, you have come from the same place. Sooner or later the Higher Self will always manifest itself.

Strange as it may seem, the fact that you have become aware of the conflict through the damage it has done to you personally is an opportunity. Pain is a message, it is not meant to be endured, it is telling you to act. You are not supposed to get used to it, you dummy. Listen to what it tells you and learn. You now have the chance to make sense of what is happening to you and to become an active participant with an objective rather than a victim. A soldier rather than a refugee. You must understand the nature of the struggle and choose your side so that your suffering can be for the understanding and control of Self, for Salvation of your Self.

Beware, if you see and understand the conflict, you can never again be the dumb slave. Imagine you come across two thugs attacking somebody at the bus stop one night. You see, you understand, how will you react. To intervene may be dangerous, to walk on means guilt and Self loathing. The unexpected knowledge of the situation has changed your life whatever you do. You will suffer whichever path you take so you may as well do the right thing. Make your suffering serve a purpose, your purpose.

To try to return to blissful ignorance is impossible. When you try, and you will, remember your list, it wasn't blissful at all. Your old life was a living hell, a delusion based on fear. Going back will not only increase your suffering it will mean you have chosen the Dark side. This is the burden of responsibility that becoming a sentient being brings. In Truth what choice do you have? It is just a question of when awareness finally moves you to action.

Most people's natural response is to help when we see another in need. We have a basic desire to help if we can. Helping others is pleasurable, it makes us feel good about ourselves. Why then do we walk on by when we see others in distress? Why do people step over an unconscious man in the street, or ignore the plight of someone being bullied? We are afraid, afraid to be noticed, afraid to get involved, afraid to accept responsibility for what seems like someone else's problems. It's our problem too. It is our learned behaviour, our experience and subsequent fear that may prevent us from helping. We must undo all the damage that has been done and have the courage to help in spite of our fear.

Having reached the Threshold of Knowing and understood its significance, you must go on. Examine your own list. If you are short on motivation you won't go far. You really have to want to change things for the better. In the ebb and flow of battles to come sometimes you will forge ahead and sometimes you will be driven back to where you started. This is quite normal, just read your list, remember what's at stake and begin again.

Remember you can be beaten but never defeated. Try, do your best, that will always be enough!

Now that you understand and wish to continue let's have a look at the opposition and some counter measures. Remember you are the weak link that the Hive must break if it is to have you. You are also Human, remember the Self loathing with which you have been programmed and have compassion for your Self.

Eden's Legacy

Self Doubt.

For me Self doubt is one of my chief foes. Even as I write I wonder at my temerity. The big job and salary are gone, the car is gone, the house is gone. I am sitting at my keyboard on a Monday morning when everyone else is doing a proper job. Nobody is interested in my work, I am an unpublished writer, that most pathetic creature, on the verge of self pity. Yet I will continue. Every time I sit and reflect on my situation I come up with the same answer. I really want to write this book. Finally I have found my place and understand my task.

We ask ourselves who am I to stand up and question the accepted norm? Who am I to be different? Who do I think I am? Marianne Williamson hits the nail on the head, with no apologies for repetition.

"Our deepest fear is not that we are inadequate; our deepest fear is that we are powerful beyond measure. It is our light, not our darkness that most frightens us. We ask ourselves who am I to be gorgeous, talented and fabulous? Actually who are you not to be? You are a child of God. Your playing small doesn't serve the world. There is nothing enlightened about shrinking so that other people won't feel insecure around you. We are born to make manifest the Glory of God that is within us; it's not just in some of us; it's in everyone. As we let our own light shine, we unconsciously give other people permission to do the same. As we are liberated from our own fear our presence automatically liberates others."

A return to love by Marianne Williamson

You are beloved of the Universe, a Child of God created in his image with the power of his love. You have the knowledge of Good and Evil and your own unique consciousness, let your Self shine, take up your crown. Master your fear.

" Be all that you can be, become what you are."

Self doubt can be a useful tool, it keeps us alert and helps in maintaining objectivity. Take your enemy and use his own force against him, an old Hive tactic. Take my own case for example, it is possible that I have made a horrible mistake. Perhaps I don't have the Self discipline needed to hold down a regular job. As long as you periodically review what you are doing and thinking with a pinch of Self doubt you will be fine.

I believe that once you have acknowledged your plight and committed your life to the fight to save your own Soul you gain access to the guidance of Heaven. When you stray, providing your motive is pure, guidance is forthcoming. So even when I go in the wrong direction I am gently guided back to the Path. This may take the form of a painful experience, it may be unrecognisable as a positive thing but in the fullness of time I see the guiding hand.

That is not to say I cannot fail. Pure motive is one of the most difficult things to achieve and even harder to maintain. Use your Self doubt to examine your motives. It is remarkable how we can deceive ourselves in these matters. Once achieved, right motive is easily distorted and unconsciously, gradually, bit by bit, it is transmuted into something unworthy. In this respect it is wise to doubt your Self.

Do not doubt your Self for stepping outside the confines of the Hive. You are unique and your methods will be unique. Being different is necessary, not a cause for Self doubt. Do not worry unduly about what others think of you, inevitably they will criticise. Use their criticism to check your progress and maintain objectivity. I have a tendency to be impulsive and sometimes when people who's opinion I respect tell me I am wrong I get annoyed and stubborn. Have the confidence to admit your errors, we all make them.

I still get depressed and lonely but at least I am trying to make sense out of my own existence. I have an objective that I can keep coming back to, my own Self fulfilment, my personal happiness and peace, my own Salvation. In this regard I am absolutely selfish. However you will soon realise that to achieve this objective, even to just strive for it, requires the sentient to strive for the rest of humanity. How can you ever enjoy Salvation if the world is full of ignorance and suffering? As long as a single Soul suffers in torment how can any of us find peace? It is impossible.

Consider the ramifications of these words, consider the scale of this terrible conflict. Small wonder we shy away from it.

Believe in your Self, nurture Self esteem and Self confidence, read about it, study it, practice it. See appendix 1.

Eden's Legacy

Low Self esteem is an extreme form of Self doubt. Low Self esteem, is the curse of modern society. Consciously or more commonly unconsciously it prevents us from wanting to even admit that we have an inner Self let alone search for it. We surround ourselves with illusions and distractions rather than face what we feel is the miserable, pathetic, weak creature at our core. The idiot offspring hidden away from the worlds unforgiving gaze.

We are frightened to assume our birthright. The incredible depth of these feelings removes our objectivity. It is pointless to tell you what a spectacular person you are, even though it is true. Like a teenage girl convinced that she is fat to the point of anorexia. Our secret beings are Spiritually anorexic. Even if you say you believe it, your behaviour will make a liar of you. Time and time again when you feel threatened you will fall back on Hive strategy, work, family and all the rest.

"No one can make you feel inferior without your consent."

Eleanor Roosevelt.

This is to be expected, plan for it. The closer you get to the truth the worse it will become. Watch for the dive into distraction. This is where the transition from Spirituality to mere religion takes place. Surreptitiously, it comes like a cunning thief, suddenly you find your Self Born Again, or building a well in Africa, be careful. Is your motive to help others or is it to distract your Self from a more difficult task? Be wary of action, reflect and meditate, await the time for action, the perfect moment.

Guilt

Guilt is the needle sharp spear with which the Hive stabs us when we become wilful. It follows close on the heels of Self doubt. These two devils, Self doubt and guilt, hound us like a pair of wolves following a wounded deer. Guilt begins in the morning when we open our eyes and dare to press the snooze button. It's there last thing at night when we consider what we have failed to do that day.

How often have you stolen a quiet moment only to be disturbed by someone noticing your inactivity? You quickly sit up pretending to be busy. At work how often have you stayed on rather than be the first to leave? How often have you taken work home just as window dressing? Why do we care so much about what other people think?

At the Monday morning diary meeting how often have you said, "My diary is pretty clear this week." My own experience of corporate life makes me shudder. I remember those meetings and feeling inadequate as I listened to what other people had scheduled for their week. I remember padding it out somewhat. We were a new group and the dynamic was volatile to say the least. We were all careful to attend because we knew that our names would be discussed and we could be assassinated or volunteered in our absence.

As I became more adept and cunning I noticed that the actual activities of the management team bore little resemblance to what was discussed at the diary meeting. Everybody embellished the truth to protect themselves from possible criticism and to make themselves feel more important. There were those who had been embellishing things for so long they actually believed that they were working flat out. They even went off sick with stress. New, younger, more naive people who replaced them were astonished at how little work there was to do. Initially I took these old lags for lazy slackers, this was unfair. It was much worse than that, they actually believed that they were overworked.

The extent to which we are able to deceive ourselves is almost limitless. Never underestimate the power of denial

For the most part our guilt is a response to what other people's perceptions of us are. Or rather what we think those perceptions are. We feel guilt if we are discovered or feel that we may be discovered doing something that does not conform to the expected norm. In this sense, guilt is a hugely powerful tool for modifying our behaviour. We just don't seem to have the confidence to be ourselves. We are always somehow conscious of being a cause of offence, of not being good enough. We always feel inadequate, threatened.

This learned guilt spurs us to ever more elaborate attempts to impress the Hive, our peers. They, or it, in turn are completely determined not only to be unimpressed but also to criticise and undermine the individual. If through our machinations we manage to achieve celebrity or the plaudits of our peers, it is an inconsequential, ephemeral, fleeting thing, of no value. It cannot satisfy, it can only mask the pain temporarily. David Attenborough once said,

"There is nothing so trivial as fame."

The Hive uses people like tissues, it screws them up and throws them away.

"The King is dead long live the King." Wheel in the next victim. The individual is expendable and can never win. There is always the newer model snapping at your heals.

Yet we crave the respect and admiration of our peers to an absolutely astonishing extent. Convinced that we alone our not enough we dismiss ourselves and don the disguise of success. Ashamed and guilty about the seemingly unlovely thing that dwells at our core we despise and mock ourselves in Self deprecation. We deflect scrutiny projecting an acceptable apparition of strength and power all the while ashamed of our hidden Self and terrified of exposure. Success, such as it is, merely makes us a focal point for the aggressive attentions of others, so in the end we settle for mediocrity and project it as success. Just enough, but not too much, inertia, limbo. Most of us don't even struggle for supremacy, we prefer our fur lined ruts.

As we grow older so we encase ourselves in layer upon layer of deceit and illusion. Our lives become devoid of satisfaction and fulfilment and contain only suffering. The suffering that signifies error and demands action. Like spawning salmon we strive against the current of the Universe and struggle blindly. We are dashed against the rocks of fate and torn by the claws of our enemies. We fight on determined, driven by mere biological instinct and the need to conquer, to succeed. Only the strong survive.

This makes for excellent fish and terrible Human beings. Salmon do not think. If they did, might they not consider turning back to the magnificent bounty of the sea? Coasting with the current at their backs they might decide to spawn along the pleasant sheltered shallows of the estuary. The hardy among them might choose the struggle to the headwaters and gravely streams of their birth. It is not a question of right and wrong but of choice. We no longer need the auto pilot of evolution and instinct but we cling to it in terror of the next level, the unknown.

Intelligent free thinking sentients reflect and choose without guilt. We are not salmon to live directed by the unreasoning scourges of evolution, ignorance, fear and guilt. If we feel guilty, if we are ashamed it should be because we hate ourselves and our cowardice. We have the innate ability to discern right from wrong, Good from Evil. This is where our guilt should come from, not from worrying about what other people think. We flee from our own Divinity and from God afraid to take up our burden. Ergo, all life is suffering.

The Universe, unable to interfere with our free Will, even though we do not want it, tries to show us the error of our ways. Sometimes when we reach a certain age, when we have suffered enough and our eyes open. We finally begin to realise our worth and begin to suspect the futility of following the Hive. We take up the heavy burden of our responsibility as sentient beings.

Mostly we do not and expire in darkness, unrealised, completely frustrating the Universe in it's attempts to make us see. We wait in the void for another turn of the wheel and perhaps a step forward until one day, inevitably we finally get the message.

Are you a bovine drone following the way of the Hive? Or are you a more Enlightened being struggling to realise your full potential? Which would you rather be? Are you embarrassed by the thought of Salvation or are you finally ready to embrace the fact that God's Divine light waits within you? Yes poor little you, magnificent you. It waits spluttering in the gloom of your life to flare up and burn away the lies and the deceit. We should all feel positively guilty when we consider this question.

Learned guilt is particularly powerful within the family. It is especially effective here because we care about what our families think about us. We all do it. Parents use it to exert control on their children and children learn to use it to control their parents. It is a terrible weapon and we use it indiscriminately. Wait until you begin to change your life, those who worry about you will use guilt to try and modify your behaviour. Everybody will try to make you feel guilty.

You will be accused of being selfish at the expense of others. Guilt will be used to make you conform and you will feel a compelling pressure to return to the Hive. This is because of the guilt you have been conditioned to feel, it may also because you may be looking for an excuse to get you off the hook and back to your cosy fur lined rut. Watch for it and remember you cannot do any real good until you have become Selfish in helping your Self. It is only then that you can begin to seriously think about others. It cannot be the other way around.

Until you begin consciously to seek Salvation for your Self, helping others is a form of illusion, a distraction, a deception.

It is only when you understand your own worth, when you realise just how precious you really are that you will start to feel the same way about others. For we are all equally precious. Remove the pernicious influence of the Hive and we see how alike we all are. We begin to understand that we are all unique pieces of the same creation.

Learned guilt is largely associated with the presence of other people. When we feel that we are not going to be discovered, when we are anonymous, our behaviour changes dramatically. Take driving for example. Your behaviour as a driver may leave something to be desired. Yes, you. Ranting at other drivers, driving too fast. Do you generally break the law? When you are driving you do, we all do. The law of the land and the laws that govern social interaction.

In your car you are separated from everything, anonymous, not accountable for your actions. Learned guilt is removed and replaced by intolerance and anger at any obstruction to our progress. Secretly we seek omnipotence, what we see as our rightful place. We are innately aware of our potential greatness. This desire is a corruption perpetrated by a lifetime of suppression and the teachings of the Hive. We have learned that we can only succeed at the expense of others through conflict. We must bide our time, conceal our innermost Self and then, crush our enemies. The reality is that in order to achieve our full potential Spiritually, to be like God, not God like, we are dependent on others not at war with them.

This secret though corrupted awareness of our own importance only surfaces when we are alone without the controlling influence of other people. The shackles fall off and we see a different animal entirely. Unfortunately, because of the injuries it has received it is not a pretty sight. The clash between our innate awareness of our own importance and the Hive's suppression of Self produces anger and frustration. Psychosis, mental anguish, pain. Sometimes we only show this side of our Self to those nearest and dearest. Hence the expression,

Gabriel Deeds

"You always hurt the ones you love." What goes on behind the closed doors of family life can be far different to the image we project for the outside world.

We live our lives the same way as we drive. Cut off from God by our own illusions and our ignorance. We behave as though there are no policemen about when in fact we are on camera. Every action is recorded and causes pain, to ourselves and to Him. We pay Him no mind, he is not part of our lives. We are obsessed with impressing the Hive and ignore Him. Our peers have more impact on our lives, they seem more real.

Since we are Self determining and free He cannot interrupt us but when we die we receive the Heavenly traffic ticket. The consequence of a lifetime speeding. I don't necessarily mean hellfire and damnation, that's a religious Hive thing, I am more inclined to the idea of rebirth. Whatever you believe you just know that you can't screw up your whole life and expect the gold watch and the keys of the City.

Guilt can be useful. Do not feel guilt as a result of breaking the Hive's rules, or even the Church's rules, the two can be the same. Rules are for guidance, not for removing the need to reflect and make conscious responsible decisions. Use your natural knowledge of the difference between Good and Evil, let your guilt cause you to reflect and modify your behaviour. Feel guilt when you hurt God in your personal relationship with Him. Feel guilt when you ignore Him, when your thoughts and actions betray his love for you. Feel guilt when you injure your Self.

We are like pressure cookers, something has to blow. This dark side of our secret nature is above all angry. All the pent up frustration pours out in seething rage. Somewhere deep in our secret core we all store up this anger which is bottled up and controlled by our fear and guilt. Fear of consequences and guilt at having these feelings and of being exposed. Where does this rage come from? It is a manifestation of our fear, we are afraid of ourselves and our responsibilities and because we are cowards we loathe ourselves.

This rage is like pus in a festering wound, it has to come out. We cannot just keep changing the bandages. No matter how clean they look the corruption is deep inside. Until it is excised and the wound cleaned we will sicken. Spiritually we rave in the delirium of our living nightmare. We won't allow anyone to touch our wounds and we can't heal ourselves. We need to understand the extent of our Self loathing and guilt and how it has come about before we can begin the terrible task of repairing the damage.

There is so much hidden pain and anger, barely concealed within each of us. Is it any wonder there is so much suffering in this world. When the anger comes, channel it against the cycle of suffering. Refuse to be used and abused, rage against the Hive not your Self or your neighbour.

Wealth

One of the most deadly foes you will face is your obsession with wealth. Most of us in the West are relatively well off. I know you would argue about that but as I said it is relative. It is not how much we have, it is the fact that so much of our time and efforts are taken up with the search for wealth. It is difficult to appreciate just what a hold this obsession has over us.

It may be the mind numbing monthly battle to balance your bank account or the burning ambition of a corporate mogul. I say mind numbing because that is exactly what happens. We become so distracted by the fight to make ends meet that we stop thinking about anything meaningful at all. Our desperate struggle to fill our wallets is the perfect camouflage for the typical Self loathing modern citizen.

It is acceptable to the Hive, what could be better for keeping the drones in order. We are so frightened of not having enough that we compete viciously against one another. We are trained to build wealth at the expense of others from birth. We may even go so far as to poison our own planet. How amazingly blind we can be. Consider though the reason for this blindness,

"There are none so blind as those who do not wish to see."

Increasingly the struggle for wealth is the real opiate of the people. It long ago superseded redundant religion. It is the same with any addiction, unless you address the underlying root cause of the unhappiness the addict will always seek oblivion by whatever means. So what makes us so unhappy, what is it that leads us to deny our sentience, even our intelligence? What would make us destroy our own planet, butcher one another over oil, allow millions to starve to death every year?

It is because we deny the Universe's love for us. It is because to admit it is to accept responsibility for our own destiny and to begin a way of life that leads us into the unknown. Away from all that is familiar and comforting to us. It is too much, too terrifying, so we hide from it and in so doing fill our lives with Self loathing. We know the Truth, that is Eden's terrible legacy, but we are afraid and for this we hate ourselves and our cowardice. We have created a living hell for ourselves and we have become accustomed to it! We don't like it, we are deeply unhappy, but it is a case of better the devil you know.

We desperately try to convince ourselves that there is only the daily grind. We measure our success in material ways that can never satisfy our need to understand that which terrifies us the most, ourselves.

Too much is never enough. I struggle with my own desire for wealth daily. Even though I claim to understand it I find it difficult to control. I am afraid of not having enough, of being poor, I was brought up to save and prosper.

"Look after the pennies and the pounds look after themselves." It took me years to resign from a well paid, deeply boring and unsatisfying job for this reason. I still fear having to go back cap in hand to find another job just like it. I fear poverty in my latter years and this kind of thing can drive us back to the Hive or more commonly stop us leaving at all. Many of us are afflicted by the acquisition habit and expend our lives trying to find a little bit more before we stop only to drop dead two weeks into retirement.

It is difficult to achieve any kind of balance with wealth. On the one hand it takes us over, on the other there is nothing so limiting as a lack of funds. If I had not endured all those years in a stultifying job I would not have had the opportunity to save my money, which in turn has given me the freedom to write and to study my Self. Secretly however I hope for financial reward as well as personal satisfaction, I want it all.

For the most part I am at peace now, but I would like the outward trappings of "success", vindication if you like. I still crave approbation and recognition. At least I am aware of it now and can keep an eye on

Eden's Legacy

my Self. The desire for wealth is a pernicious weed that can spring up and choke the aspiring Seeker.

"It is easier for a camel to go through the eye of a needle than for a rich man to enter the Kingdom of Heaven."

Mathew 17 verse 24.

How many of us could sell up everything and give the proceeds away? Few, too few, the best that most of us can hope for is to be aware of our failings, to be truly honest about ourselves and hope for mercy. We cannot find Salvation alone we can only seek it diligently and wait for help when we falter.

God is well used to stuffing fat camels through small holes, the least we can do is diet!

Property

Related to wealth, our love affair with property is another manifestation of the same obsession with material possessions. We blabber endlessly on about our houses. Kitchens, patios, decks, extensions and how big our gardens are. The state of the property market and the value of our houses seem to be the only thing we talk about these days. Its one of those safe subjects that we all talk about at parties when we are trying to put one over on those people that we don't know that well but who we need to impress anyway.

Your house is your home. If you are lucky enough to have one or rent one be glad for what you have and think of those who have nothing. Your house may seem innocuous enough but like anything material it can become an all consuming objective. In struggling for that house that you have always wanted you are diverted from the important things in life. You are able to push those annoying thoughts of Self well into the long bushes of your mind.

Ultimately your house should be a home for your family. The home is what is important not the bricks and mortar. There are many good homes in the cardboard box shanty towns of our world. Though they may have little material wealth they may have much more than we do.

Beverly Hills or the slums of our largest Cities? Ironically, there is no clear correlation between material wealth and happiness. Do the best that you can for your family in building a home for them and try not to worry about competing for bigger and better all the time.

How much time and effort do you put into your property? How much time and effort do you put into building a loving home? Make a clear distinction between the two and always remember that everything you create, good and bad, will come from your Self. If you neglect your Self you will be unable to build a happy loving home no matter how hard you try or how wealthy you are.

So how do we fight this pervasive desire for wealth and property? The primary defence lies always in awareness. Being aware of the problem and the danger is at least half the battle. Wealth in itself is not a bad thing, it is a question of the priority that you give it in your life. Any good religion will advise you on how to combat your desire but first you must be aware of it and understand your Self.

Work

In terms of Self defence, how is work a threat? How can we defend ourselves from it?

The great work ethic, that pillar of our society, is one of the Hive's greatest weapons in the struggle to suppress us from seeking freedom. A life's work can be a miracle or it can be a nightmare. It is a nightmare when used as a distraction from Self. It is another opiate of the people.

When the individual is happily seeking Self, then work can have meaning and real power. Each of us has gifts which when properly realised can be used to improve and enhance our world.

For the most part we equate work with survival, we have bills to pay and families to feed. How convenient. We work to live instead of living to work. Once again the Hive within us confuses goals and objective. Paying the bills, the daily grind becomes our sole reason for existence and obliterates our objective, personal Salvation.

As a distraction it is perfect. It is acceptable to the Hive and provides us with a mirage to follow. The shimmering oasis of our twisted concept of success. Career, respect, power, wealth. Or perhaps just a pay packet. Most of us settle for just enough to maintain a thin veneer of respectability. We quietly expend our lives doing the mundane, routine chores that pay the bills. We find our opiate in family or religion or some kind of hobby. We die a little every day on the golf course and in the garden centre seeking happiness but always without peace. The Hive buys us two a penny, we sell Self cheap!

The first step is to recognise the reality of your situation whatever it is. If you find after careful investigation that your work is incompatible with your objective then change it. For the most part this is not necessary however. Your objective of personal Salvation may be established without a change in career. Bills do have to be paid, families do have to be fed. These are legitimate responsibilities for most of us and satisfying them is a goal that leads to the objective. An honest days work never hurt anyone and helps to keep the feet firmly on the ground. Christ was a carpenter.

The important thing is how your work is prioritised in your mind. Is your work a goal or is it the objective?

Family (See also social interaction chap 12)

Your family poses one of the greatest threats to your search for Self. It does so in two ways.

1. Family provides good cover for avoiding Self.
2. Your family exert more influence over you than anyone else.

To devote your Self to your family can be an important act of Self sacrifice on the road to Enlightenment. For those who understand or are learning about the nature and importance of their own Self, having a family can help them on their journey to Salvation. Ideally, one should come before the other. In the paradox of being Self centred and Self sacrifice the simple truth is that until you own your Self you cannot sacrifice it. You simply cannot give what you do not possess.

Anything that we attempt to build will be illusory and add to the distracting layers we build around ourselves in hiding from Self. No matter how hard we try or how much we seem to give ultimately we are going up a blind alley and will have to retrace our steps sooner or later.

In an ideal world we would have our families after having at least begun the search for Self. The reality is different however. Most of us have families by the time we come to search for Self. This reality means that many of us unconsciously choose to use our families as an excuse to avoid assuming our responsibilities to Self. We can even grow to resent our families seeing them as an impediment, the ball and chain that prevents us from growing. What a neat way to avoid our own responsibility to Self.

It is easy and acceptable to seem to devote ones life to the family. The Hive beams down on such loyal drones because they faithfully repeat the cycle of suffering. God knows how much time and effort raising a family takes. If you have your family before your Self is discovered the journey is much harder. Not impossible, but harder. This is something we should teach our children. However, obstacles are made to be overcome.

So you have your family and you need to explore your Self. How is your family a threat? Your whole life is tied up with your family and providing for them, they way you think and act, your entire existence revolves around your family. The relationships you have formed within your family circle are deep and powerful but as yet there is no hint of your need to explore Self.

No matter how well you know your family or how well they know you, the search for your Self is something that they will be unaware of. How could they know when you scarcely realise it your Self? To begin the search will mean change and it would be a strange thing if your family didn't notice a change in you. How they react will have a very strong influence on you. Their opinions and feelings mean a lot to you and this can make you vulnerable.

It would be unreasonable to expect them to understand what you struggle to understand. How can you explain it to them so that their reaction will not damage your resolve to continue? (You could try buying them a copy of this book). This is almost impossible and as I have already said earlier on, it is probably wiser to keep much of your journey private until you are more comfortable with it your Self.

Assuming that you will not be able to fully explain, how can you deal with their natural confusion and possibly their attempts to alter your behaviour? Firstly be aware of your vulnerability to the bond that exists between you and the power of their influence over you. If you are aware of the problem then you can deal with it if you give your Self the time and space. Families, time and space are words that are scarcely ever seen in the same sentence.

In the chaos of family life it is all too easy to fall back into the comforting embrace of the Hive because of the very real constraints on time and energy. If I was to say to a working Mum with two kids,

" Take some time to get to know your Self," she would probably laugh in my face. If I was to say to an overworked and harassed Dad,

" Have you ever thought about meditation?" Well you know what he will say, don't you? Assuming that you get a moment of clarity in which you decide to make Self a priority, rare enough in itself, how will the family react? How can you protect your self from their reaction? By being ready for the blow, by expecting it and by controlling your reaction to it.

The blow may be a simple comment or it could be a full blown row about how you have changed, how selfish you have become. Your new found need for time and space may be the cause of envy or a feeling that you are slacking, not pulling your weight. By being prepared for the blow you can in some measure understand it and so discount it. At the same time you know that this is part of the cycle of conflict through which the Hive will try to reclaim you, do not enter into conflict, break the cycle through your awareness of it.

Your family will inflict wounds on you that no other could, Self doubt and guilt are covered elsewhere in this book but there will be pain, a lot of pain. Your family know which buttons to press and because they may not understand your journey and be unaware of the whole process, they will to some extent, be the Hive's tools. Doggedly concentrate on your Self first and foremost, be ruthless and determined. You can do nothing for anyone else until you are on the way to Salvation for your Self.

Prayer

I pray a lot, not in the religious sense, but as in talking to a loved mentor and friend. Forget the idea of public prayer, I am a deeply private person and prayer comes to me in solitude. Public worship is about sharing and communion at best, at worst it is a matter of habit or illusion, a Hive thing. In this journey into the unknown there are few charts to hearten and encourage us. We must truly go boldly where no one has gone before.

Spirituality and Science are entirely compatible in this respect. For the unknown and what we do not understand there is Spirituality. Our Spirituality gives us the courage to explore and through Science and our intelligence we come to understanding, awareness. Since the Universe is infinite, there will always be new frontiers to explore. There will always be Spirituality and there will always be Science. Both expand side by side as we become Enlightened.

I believe that we are made in the image of God, we have a fragment of Him within us. Your personal beliefs are immaterial. Even if you claim to believe in nothing you have the indisputable evidence of your Self. Communicate with the Divine within your Self, with your God, your creator or the Universal Consciousness. Open a channel and use it regularly. Call it prayer if it suits you.

"In my Father's house there are many mansions."

I personally try to follow Christ's example and derive great comfort from communication with him. Without this personal conduit I would have no chance at all of attempting or surviving the journey to Salvation. As my friend I try not to hurt or upset him and he has made it abundantly clear what hurts and upsets him. This knowledge and our friendship has a dramatic effect on my behaviour, even, or should I say, especially my thoughts, which remember are the precursor to all actions.

Through prayer I can find release, catharsis. Christ is the shoulder I cry on, he is always there for me arms outstretched no matter what I have done. I have no secrets from Christ, no need to hide or pretend. He coaxes me forward towards understanding and awareness. He is the glimmer of light at the end of the tunnel through which I will find Enlightenment.

In my prayer I am conscious of a two way process. I must listen and give, as well as ask. I constantly find my Self asking for more or less the same things. The wisdom and strength to actively seek Enlightenment. and lately I have also asked God to give my writing the power to move people and help them change their lives for the better. I pray that it will be so. The important thing is to try.

Eden's Legacy

It is good and wise to prepare for the struggle ahead. By using your skills and intelligence you can cushion the effect of the tactics that will be used against you by the Hive. However you will not always succeed. When you are caught out, as inevitably you will be, you will have your Self to fall back on. Your awareness of the conflict and your place in it will put the wounds that will be inflicted on you into context. Your clear objective and goals will always mean that you suffer for a purpose, the only one that matters, the realisation of your Self.

Resources, see also appendix 1 and 2.

Books – The Road Less Travelled.
Movies – Billy Elliot, The Game.

Chapter 12, Social interaction

We are social creatures whether we like it or not. The primate within us is incredibly dependent on the other people around it, almost to the exclusion of all else. Our social status, our connections, our influence, our success is measured in terms of how we are regarded by our peers. In general, nothing has so much power over us as the instinctive and learned bonds that hold us together as a species. This is our fundamental strength and our crippling weakness.

As a species on our planet we are unsurpassed biologically. As the Hive measures things we are top of the evolutionary tree because of our cohesion and vigour. We fight well together because we are able to coordinate our efforts. This is due to the way in which we interact socially. The more cohesive, coordinated and team orientated the more successful in conflict. This is bad news for Self.

Man terrorises and exploits the whole planet. The glory of the Roman Empire is renowned, and yet, ultimately it failed, as do all Empires eventually. Pax Romana, pax Britannica, pax Americana any kind of peace is of absolutely no use whatsoever to the Hive. Our evolution and the instincts inbred into us over the millennia drive us remorselessly to conflict. Conflict is the fuel that feeds natural selection, but we can change, we must change.

We are not soldier ants we are people, we are not merely expendable drones fighting for the greater good as dictated by those in authority. Somewhere along our evolutionary path we developed the capacity to reach a sentient level. This spark of Divinity has been with us a long, long time. Since the first Neanderthal threw the bones to bless the hunt. Where it came from has absorbed and distracted us for centuries. Science and religion have been in conflict over the subject for ever. There is that word again, conflict.

Any civilised society that treats the individual as we do, based on the social structure of a troop of baboons, is in trouble. One troop is more organised than another so it prospers and multiplies passing on the social tendencies that led it to success. Eventually, everything the troop does is based on the greater good and the suppression of the individual. Great, but what of sentience, what of Spirituality and the individual?

Eden's Legacy

As a species we are definitely in deep trouble, doomed in fact, lets be honest. We can't go on like this. We are not baboons and we cannot live like baboons no matter how successful we might appear to be. This suppression of the unique sentient individual within us leads us to neurosis, schizophrenia, madness. We are both primate and sentient trapped in a primordial evolutionary loop that keeps going around and around and around. This is the cycle of suffering, the great wheel of life which has become an instrument of torture, a rack upon which we groan and sob in perpetual agony.

Lets see if we can shed some light on the problem and finally see things as they really are. Before our biological success destroys us lets see if we can move on to the next level in the evolutionary game. At the moment we are embarrassing ourselves as a sentient species. If there is intelligent life out there among the stars, they must be very concerned about their human neighbours from Hell. If we ever demonstrate the capacity for intergalactic travel our neighbours might consider galactic pest control. Ants are very interesting in the garden but when they come into the house something has to be done.

The desire to belong

We are born into a family, part of a community or Tribe, we are seldom alone especially in our formative years. As children we play together and form small groups or gangs naturally avoiding being seen to be alone. To be alone, separated from the group is to be vulnerable, the thought of it fills us with horror. All our lives we long for the words,
"Do you want to be in my gang?"

To stay within a group we will sacrifice much of our own individuality, we will adapt our behaviour and adhere to group rules no matter how abhorrent they may be. Witness the Nazi death camps or the killing fields of Cambodia, Siberia, Angola, Bosnia, Rwanda, Chechnya, Iraq or the Congo. We do like our killing fields don't we? All such atrocities are committed by ordinary people like you and I. Ordinary people who feel that they must belong whatever the cost. We crave the feeling of belonging and the comfort and security that it brings. We seek the embrace of the group and then fear the consequences of openly expressing ourselves.

Gabriel Deeds

    We know that this is wrong. Deep in our subconscious we know that this behaviour is abhorrent but we do it anyway. It's a damn site easier and safer than thinking for your Self. This cowardly behaviour breeds Self loathing on a massive scale and ironically this can make us even more fiercely protective of the group.
"If I can put up with it so can you." Or,
"If its good enough for me, its good enough for you." Or,
"It's always been this way."
    Those who live outside the group or those who would leave the group are treated as lower forms of life. At a very basic level, survival of the fittest mentality means that outsiders may be attacked, indeed must be attacked lest they grow too strong and pose a threat. This is the very nature of discrimination, racial, religious, sexual whatever kind you care to mention.
    I do not necessarily mean that the group will literally make a physical attack, although it can and often does. The group has many powerful methods of enforcing its code. The horrible pressure applied by peer groups in the playground are well known to all of us. Which of us has not suffered in the school break and which of us has not turned a blind eye to the torture inflicted on others? Who enjoys their first drink or their first cigarette? Never underestimate the power of peer pressure and the corrosive effect it can have on your life. Recognise the damage it has already done especially to your Secret Being.
    Discrimination in all its forms is Tribal in nature. An old man pulls out in front of you and you curse,
"Silly old bugger." A man makes a fuss about a cold and the ladies all shout,
 " All men are babies." A woman makes her husband wait outside a lingerie shop and he rolls his eyes at the guy standing beside him. We are always seeking to build alliances, find the common ground. It is usually at the expense of somebody else. How often are we derogatory or disparaging about another person for no particular reason? Look at the media, so negative, so delighted to stick the knife in. Remember the media is just feeding our appetite for conflict, we are the mob in the colosseum and we like blood.
    The more obvious the difference the more extreme our reaction. Race and religion speak eloquently for themselves. None of us are

immune from this discriminatory behaviour, the best we can do, if we are honest is be aware of it and control it. After all, ironically it is something all people have in common.

Shocking as it may seem this primordial behaviour still drives much of our thinking and many of our actions even as adults. We love to pigeonhole and judge our fellow man,
" And what do you do for a living?"
" Where do you live?"
" Is that your car?"

There are gender related differences but generally we treat everybody as a competitor to be threat assessed and then attacked, used or ignored depending on our superficial enquiries. The first step is to belong to a powerful group, to compete within its hierarchy, rise within its ranks and if required join a more powerful group. To be alone is an anathema. We have an innate phobia of being excluded and will do almost anything to stay within the Tribe.

Indeed the benefits to the individual cannot be overlooked. Being part of a team is a stimulating and empowering thing. On a simple level two people can lift more than double the load an individual can manage. On a more complex level a civilisation can elevate the ideals of education, culture and Spirituality or it can become a Third Reich. It is a powerful and dangerous thing, as we succeed so we usually end up looking down at somebody else. Our pre programmed need for conflict undermines any peaceful society until conflict is rekindled.

The downside of this powerful group dynamic is the diminishment of the individual and worse, the abrogation of individual responsibility. The famous excuse,

"I was only following orders," is not an excuse at all it's the prelude to tragedy, disaster and conflict. So it is that all great Empires fail and crumble eventually as the individual becomes less and less important in the eyes of society and in our own hearts. It does not come about in the individual decision to shoot someone because you have been told to. It starts long before that in the little things.

It starts when you see something which is wrong and tell your Self, "What can I do on my own?" When your school lays off a teacher because of budget cuts and your child's class size increases, what do you do? When the local hospital closes a ward, what do you do? When the

Gabriel Deeds

Town council decides to consolidate the local library into a bigger one further away, what do you do? You tell your Self that you cannot make a difference on your own and do nothing. You diminish your Self and in so doing open the door to apathy and cynicism. Ask your Self,

"If not you, then who?"

These great Empires start out well, for example,

"We hold these truths to be self-evident, that all men are created equal, that they are endowed by their Creator with certain inalienable Rights, that among these are Life, Liberty and the pursuit of Happiness."

The very words make the hair stand up on the back of the neck. New rules for a new kind of social interaction based on the rights of the individual, such power, such promise. Yet even here, over time the Hive has twisted and corroded the shining ideal. It recovered from the huge body blow such Enlightened thinking dealt it and gave us Vietnam and Guantanimo Bay.

On kicking the French out of Vietnam, Ho Chi Minh addressed the people after the long struggle. Unaware of the even more bitter struggle to come. His first words to a joyful nation,

"We hold these truths to be self evident, that all men are created equal, that they are endowed by their Creator with certain inalienable Rights,"

In a truly bitter, bitter, irony, Ho Chi Minh felt an ideological kinship with the Americans who had thrown off the British yoke and created a new order. He asked for seeds, tractors and teachers, he got hot lead and napalm. The British, the French, the German, it matters not, every Empire is as good or as bad as its individual citizens. We must be eternally vigilant against the insidious, caustic, interminable drip, drip, drip of the Hive's poison. It can and does undermine and even destroy our most precious ideals.

We must learn to realise that the individual Self is the basic building block of civilisation and for the proper evolution of mankind. Until we each of us recognise the dramatic part that we play in the struggle between Good and Evil and take our responsibility seriously the cycle of evolutionary conflict will continue. If the quality of the individual unit is neglected then we will always struggle in ignorance and fear. There is no check to the Hives constant corrupting influence.

When we lock up our enemies, or just those that might be our enemies, without charge or legal representation, then, we become that which we seek to destroy. When we cross our neighbour's borders, seeking revenge and profit, we destroy our own civilisation, built in patient toil. We spit on what our ancestors built in their fight against fascism and injustice. In our emotional righteous indignation we are united in our anger. We are caught up in the joy of destroying the enemy, we are corrupted to tyranny and recruited to the banner of the Hive.

Every time you turn a blind eye or undermine an opponent, even in the most petty detail, not only are you damaging your fellow man, you are corroding your Self and your own fitness for use in construction. Regardless of your religious beliefs such negative energy ties us to the wheel of suffering. The positive energy of education, tolerance, and an open mind, give us direction, fulfilment and peace. We have to learn to live like sentient beings and accept the role that we each must play.

Until each individual chooses to master themselves and search for the freedom of Enlightenment our collective societies will only reflect the flaws found in each person. We must start with ourselves and work to tip the balance so that understanding and mastery of Self are established as part, not just of the occasional person's ideology, but of our whole world. This is the struggle that we must begin, this is the side that we must belong to.

If you begin to make changes in your life, assuming personal responsibility and improving your outlook and actions you will be attacked and undermined by the groups you belong to. Recognise these attacks for what they are, the Hive reacting to you for a change, learn to watch for them. Remember the powerful effect they will have on you because of your conditioning. You are not infallible, watch for conscious or unconscious attempts to return to the fold. Even St Peter denied Christ when challenged by the Hive and we are not Saints. Allow for lapses, expect them. Allow for them, but be vigilant.

Even so you will have to toughen up. You will become despondent, and angry, you will try to lay off the responsibility. You must deal not only with the attacks on you, you must control your own counter attack. Once they get under your skin you will be tempted to engage the enemy. In the heat of battle, as the red mist subsides, your foes crushed, elation will give way to the sudden and shocking realisation that you are back in the pack. Once more you are a successful combatant in the Hive's arena and it will feel good, so good.

At this exact moment of realisation, you will be tempted to take the easy way.

Remember the Threshold of Knowing, remember why you started, remember what you are trying to do. So you've been suckered, laugh it off, chalk one up to the Dark Side, that doesn't mean you give up. Learn your lesson and start again, all the wiser. As you progress you will begin to understand other peoples emotions and actions and so naturally your own will be modified. When someone attacks you in anger, because you understand their fear, your own anger is dissipated and the cycle is broken.

So now you feel pretty good, you turned the other cheek, you didn't rise to the bait. So what if he's a stockbroker and drives a Porsche, he's probably on valium, in debt and on the verge of divorce. You on the other hand are on the Path to Salvation, a Spiritual Warrior, a superior being. Wham! Again you're back in the pack. You beat him, you just used a different weapon, chalk up another one to the Dark Side. Your fellow humans are not the enemy, the enemy is within your Self. The Hive exists in you, in every individual. You are fighting for your Self and for every other oppressed soul that you may previously have viewed as the opposition.

When you are confused and frustrated, unsure of the way ahead, meditate, pray, reflect. When you feel threatened and angry, when you are in the grip of any strong emotion, avoid reacting. Take the time to regroup, reflect and meditate in peace and solitude, regain your equanimity. Imagine you are moving through a crowded room with a tray full of your favourite Waterford crystal wine glasses. You move cautiously, slowly, keeping a careful eye on your own movements and those of the people and things around you. These glasses are like your equanimity, cherish and protect it.

Try to determine what it is that has upset you and why. Often, you will find that the problem will dissipate in the process. Maintain the necessary space and time for the use of these tools at all costs. Remember you do belong, not to a troop of baboons but to the Universal Consciousness. You need to think big, you are part of the brotherhood and sisterhood of humanity.

I find people, even individuals very distracting. I find I am constantly trying to give or receive signals, trying to guess what they are thinking or what they like and dislike. I know that I do this in anticipation of attack. As a result of my schooling I treat everyone as a threat. To me it is almost overwhelming physically and mentally. I feel buried, unable to cope with the intensity of human interaction. I seek solitude, anonymity. Its like unplugging, stepping off the round about. It is only then that my thoughts coalesce taking form in my mind so that I can convert them into action.

Frustratingly, I soon find that I need the company of my fellow Humans. I am distressed, bored, lacking in inspiration and find myself seeking out their company. The truth is I need both solitude and communion in balanced measures to remain sane and to progress.

Remember, where ever possible use the Hive's tactics against it. Take your conditioning and training and consciously use them in your struggle. Recognise your own need to belong and the benefits it can bring and choose more appropriate groups. Retaining your Spiritual independence and responsibility, seek out other like minded souls. You may be surprised at what you find. Draw comfort if you can, it may strengthen you and hearten you in those dark times that will come, but remember the siren call of the Hive. Do not be deceived. The Hive loves a crowd.

Solitude

Solitude is necessary for calm and clear reflection. It is possible to reflect even in a crowded public place, but it is more difficult. That is precisely why we hate being alone. We all of us have a private place in our heads where none may go except us. Nobody knows what we are thinking, except, remember, the Universal Consciousness.

For me this is expressed as God, for others, who knows? Even an atheist must recognise the spark of sentience within. It is another facet of Self for we have more than one. As soon as we are alone, these facets, physical, emotional, intellectual and Spiritual begin to debate, and we hate it, because we feel inadequate, scared, surrounded, overwhelmed.

How these various facets of Self interact, particularly, the chain of command as it were, the pecking order, is what Enlightenment or Salvation is all about. Other people impose their physical presence on us as well as their mental energy. It is impossible to overstate the distracting effect we have on one another in our thoughts words and actions. A little solitude is the simple solution. It is both a defensive mechanism and a weapon.

It can be a form of recreation, a soothing bath with a good book or a long walk along the beach. We do become weary of company from time to time, we all need our privacy. Remember your time management skills. Once we have cleared our heads and acclimatised ourselves to being alone then we can take things a step further. We can begin the task of unravelling our lives and picking out the way ahead. At this point we usually declare a sudden need for company or distraction. Before things get too heavy we scuttle back to the other Baboons. We are terrified of solitude.

Until we understand and love ourselves enough and realise just how powerful we really are we can't cope with solitude. We have to be reintroduced to ourselves, gradually, bit by bit. You can use my template as outlined in this book or find one of your own, just look, investigate. Solitude is a vital requirement for your progress along the road to Enlightenment. As you become accustomed to it and as your independence and confidence grows, you will value it, crave it, more and more.

Use it well, but remember too much solitude too soon can unbalance the mind and divorce you from reality. Balance is the key.

Isolation

To a large extent you must forgo the luxury and comfort of the group. This is a lonely way and there is danger within the pack no matter how benign it may seem. Should you take Holy orders and retire to a Monastery you will find devout, Holy people, you will also find intolerance, bigotry and petty adherence to trivial ritual. This is the nature of the Hive and it surreptitiously stifles the infant seeker. The loneliness of our responsibility is a stark realisation, and has broken many millions of would be seekers. It is hard to feel alone.

To feel alone is a terrible thing, not to be underestimated, but we are not alone. If we can foreswear the ways of the Hive and struggle towards the light we join a band of unseen warriors living and dead. They represent the hope of human kind, they have joined with the Universal Consciousness. This Universal Consciousness is ever ready to aid those truly on the Path. It may not seem obvious or even apparent, we often ask for the wrong things, but we are not alone, help is at hand.

Each of us is like a probe heading into deep uncharted space. Sent out alone, as isolated emissaries, gathering knowledge and understanding, becoming more aware as we struggle along. Each of us can add to the ever expanding pool of the Universal Consciousness. It is not a static thing, it grows as each probe begins to function and send telemetry. As each one stutters into life and begins to glow like an incandescent flame, a new star in the Dark sky, so all Heaven rejoices and takes a step forward.

All true but of little help to the Seeker who feels alone and deserted. The depths of this despair are epitomised in the words of Christ as he hung from the pitiless cross,

" Father…, Father, why hast thou forsaken me?"

Christ himself has endured the agony of our legacy. He chose to fight and to die, to show us the Way. He has suffered as we suffer and in so doing leads the way, hands held out, waiting in the happy throng of those who have endured and succeeded and now wait anxiously for us.

Realise that the Universal Consciousness quivers with hope and the anticipation that you will one day stagger to the door your mission completed. You're new mission, to help all those who struggle behind. You are not alone.

Socialise

If you are thinking that I lead a boring existence, well you may be right. I certainly don't feel bored. My life is akin to something from Lord Of The Rings believe me. I fight demons everyday. If you feel the need for the traditional high life of wine, women/men and song, well fine.

Socialise, forget your troubles for a while, take a break, have a dance, indulge your Self a little. Just remember what is real and what is illusion.

There is a difference between blowing off steam and hiding. The bars and clubs are full of tortured souls seeking oblivion in sex, drugs and alcohol. In general it is best to avoid anything that will alter your conscious state chemically. You don't need it to have fun, you do need it to anaesthetise your Self and avoid your responsibilities. Moderation and vigilance at all times.

People come to the Threshold of Knowing when the time is right for them. If you are fortunate enough to have a kindred spirit you are lucky indeed. Be circumspect and keep an eye on your motive for talking to them. Always honestly ask your Self, why am I doing this? I would say that if you have a handful of true friends in this life you are well off. My circle of friends changed completely when I started out. Gradually I met new people on the way and became less tolerant of old relationships. Many of these were mere acquaintances that I cultivated to seem popular or because they were useful or out of duty. You only find out who your true friends are, if you have any, when the chips are down.

Even though I have close friends and family my quest has been an intensely private one until now. It is only the need to try to help others that makes me speak of it now. This action is derived from the desire to save my Self in the only way possible, Self sacrifice born of empathy and compassion.

Ironically we can only save ourselves by sacrificing ourselves.

Relationships

I have already touched on some of this in the family threat section, it needs repeating. The words and actions of others cannot destroy what you are building, but they can put some serious dents in it. Apart from your Self the other main force arrayed against you will be the other people in your life. Everybody from the total stranger to your nearest and dearest. Remember you are a social animal even if you think you are not.

Other people have a profound effect on your actions, thoughts and words. Nearly everything you do is related in some way to the people around you.

Eden's Legacy

Acknowledge it now.

If you take any of this seriously it is going to affect you and your behaviour noticeably. Initially, those closest to you will see change first. They may already be aware of your unhappiness, unease and frustration. You may be having problems with relationships as a result of these feelings already. If you feel able, talk to them about these feelings openly. Bring them with you a little way so that they understand at least what you are feeling and that you are trying to improve things.

As I said be wary of discussing your innermost thoughts. These are still forming in your mind, it may be years before you understand them your Self. Be strong and do this bit alone for now. If you are in some measure successful those closest to you will notice a calmer more approachable you and be pleased. However even if they express curiosity be careful of going too far in trying to explain your journey. Be wary of the "soap box" syndrome. I have a tendency, in my enthusiasm, to blather on about my new found wisdom. We should always regard ourselves as novices, more inclined to listen than to speak. Two ears one mouth, we should listen twice as much as we speak.

In this respect those nearest and dearest are actually the ones who can do you the most damage. They have a preconceived perception of you and won't necessarily like to see you change. They can damage you, not out of malice but merely as a result of their conditioning and their concern for you. We never see ourselves as others do. Even the closest confidant sees only a snapshot of the real you. If you suddenly start talking about scary forbidden subjects you are going to get a negative response. This is disappointing and discouraging and remember your own susceptibility to other people and their perception of you.

It is better to employ a little Hive camouflage and work quietly within your Self until you are stronger and wiser. No matter how much you desire respect and approbation you will not get what you want from other people only from your Self.

Stay concealed in so far as far as you can, but remember, your actions are now directed by your desire for Salvation so you will occasionally have to stand out. However you need not make a point of it. Standing out from the crowd is very wearing and it can lead to a bit of an ego trip. You will probably find your Self feeling a little smug, proud.

We love to feel superior and you are only human after all, keep an eye on it.

"Pride goes before a fall."

Most of us are less fortunate in the closeness of our personal relationships. I would go so far as to say this is the norm. We seldom discuss any of the things that are truly important in our lives. How can we when we refuse to acknowledge them ourselves? Pathetic isn't it? So any interaction will be on a superficial level within the illusory part of our lives. It cannot kill your Spirituality but it can grind it down.

At best this interaction will manifest itself as pleasure in your improved behaviour towards those around you. You have a right to expect this from your family, but much will depend on how your new thinking effects your old life. Even if you have uncovered the illusory nature of our modern lives others may not be so fortunate. Indeed they are probably as yet unaware even of the conflict in which you are now engaged.

At worst their reaction will take the form of open hostility, sarcasm and cynicism will flow like water. Your actions will seem like a rejection of what others have learned to tolerate with the implicit criticism of them. Whether from colleagues at work or from close family and friends it can magnify Self doubt, which is the real problem. Remember your personal rights page 123. Treat this negativity for what it is, the Hive reacting to you for a change.

This is a sign of success.

For me the change was a dramatic one, I felt the need to violently throw off the yoke of my illusion. I hated my old life with a vengeance, I was happy to drop it and walk away. Let me say at this point that I am single, a wife and children would have changed things dramatically. I think I have always known that I would need to be free, I just didn't know why.

Partners in general are deeply distracting and require a great deal of mental and physical energy. Somehow I knew I had unfinished business that would require every ounce of energy that I could muster. The other thing of course is that this journey is absolutely guaranteed to change you in a very fundamental way. It is more difficult if you are constantly concerned with the effects of your behaviour on someone close to you and indeed their effect on you. It is scarcely fair to expect another to watch you change in ignorance of your motives and yet it is almost impossible to explain. There is also a great risk of damaging your fragile Self confidence should they react in a negative way.

The Hive has made me a solitary person. I used to think this was a curse, now I believe it to be a boon. I suspect it may even have been preordained, part of my training. The Hive tries to cripple me by isolating me and the Universal Consciousness uses this negativity to make me more aware of my Self, more independent. Sometimes we doubt that there is a creator and sometimes we get a little glimpse of the great plan to reassure us.

If you are not solitary find comfort with a friend or a loved one who can share your enjoyment. Remember that your quest is a personal, private thing. Be wary of trying to share it with anyone. I have found it very difficult to express to another and I find the experience can be disappointing. People seldom truly understand the nature of the conflict you are engaged in. They are inevitably embarrassed, or sceptical or just plain bored. I have even caught my Self trying to convert friends, be careful. Awareness comes to us only when it is time.

What I was really looking for was approbation, acceptance, the comfort of my own pack. I wanted, still do, to be admired and respected, to know I was doing the right thing. This cannot be! Sometimes you will do the wrong thing. These are uncharted waters, on the map it says,

"Here there be dragons."

Imagine the great explorer Captain Cook blundering through the deadly shoals of the Great Barrier Reef. He had no reliable charts, no one to follow. The crew must have thought him insane. Years at sea, thousands of miles from home, on a hostile shore without charts or anyone to share his burden. Daily they risked death and disease. This is the kind of Spiritual independence that you will need to continue. You will need to be your own navigator, Captain, hero.

I have avoided the complexities of relationships by staying single. I am no monk rather I crave simplicity, calm and clarity. It suits my personality and the nature of my task. I believe that because of my childhood and schooling and the damage the Hive inflicted on me I am singularly inept when it comes to women. When I fall in "love," I fall hard. It takes me a long time to recover from the devastation. The Universal Consciousness has used my ineptitude to make it possible for me to stay single and to divert my energy to the study of Self. Part of the great unfathomable plan? Perhaps. It may be that at some point, probably when I am least expecting it, I will be pole axed by cupid. I try to keep an open mind.

    The point is that one comes before the other. Awareness of Self, Self confidence and the understanding of the individual's responsibility to seek Enlightenment should ideally come first. If it does not, well look at the divorce statistics. How much suffering do we endure as a result of inappropriate relationships? Sort out your relationship with your Self before you contemplate inflicting your Self on someone else. We too often use other people to hide behind or to shore up our inadequacies. We don't like to be alone or perceived as "gay" or unusual so we get hitched. We all know that favourite Hive question,
"Do you have a girlfriend, or boyfriend?"

    How often has that one made you uncomfortable just because you don't have a partner? How often do we lie about that one? Why do we feel uncomfortable about not having a partner? Do you go out for dinner alone, or to the movies or to the dreaded party? Why should it be so difficult to be alone? It is because we are not content with ourselves. We fear being seen to be alone and yet is there anything more unhappy or lonely than a bad relationship. (American Beauty, appendix 2)

    Compound a bad relationship with children and you see what a powerful Hive tool relationships are. Totally distracting to the search for Self, energy sapping and ideal for turning out damaged clones. After all now that you have been pressured into a relationship you gotta have kids. People might think you were shooting blanks or barren! Oh, and don't forget hormones, what would the Hive do without testosterone and oestrogen and all the other hormones that regulate us? There go your next twenty years or so. The simple fact of over population turns our world into a cauldron of conflict and suffering. If you pack too many baboons into a small space what else would you expect?

    I am ill equipped to deal with relationships and suspicious of the whole process. This is my unique situation and although it may seem a little extreme and has a very definite downside I prefer it to the chaos and agony of "love". I have recently recovered sufficient Self confidence to realise that I need to concentrate more time and effort on friends and their needs. I have been too much of a recluse and now I am enjoying the process of cultivating friendship and exploring friends old and new. The need for social interaction is a something each of us has to work out in our own way.

Practically speaking, by the time we begin to be aware of our sentience and our Self most of us have acquired a partner and children. I am going to stick my neck out here and say that I believe this is largely a Hive thing. We are driven by our biological Hive needs and peer pressure before we even begin to become aware of our Higher Self. So it is necessary to both explore Self and fulfil obligations to your family.

It is difficult for me to advise those with partners and families but on the whole I would suggest caution. You will be changing in a positive way and the effects of this will benefit your family. You are not deceiving them but shielding them and protecting your Self. We are well used to deceit, you are once again using a Hive tactic to positive ends. If the time comes when you feel the need to make dramatic changes in your life things might be different.

We all need to compromise to some extent but there are also times when absolute single-mindedness is required. Some would call it ruthlessness, it is a fine line. Reflect on this,

You may find that the people who cross the finish line with you, if there are any, are not the ones you started out with.

Take a few minutes and compile a list of all the people that you know and love. I don't mean the ones you should love but don't. I mean all the people that you really love, your true friends. The people that you could talk to about the issues raised in this book without them thinking you were crazy or being embarrassed. It is not a long list believe me. I managed six and I am well pleased. Be brave and honest, most people would score a big fat zero. See how many you can add to your list.

Remember, before you can proceed you need to recognise how bad things are. This may feel bad but it is a positive thing, something that you can build on. Enter their names below.

Gabriel Deeds

My <u>true</u> friends,

1.
2.
3.
4.
5.
6.

    My family, were less than pleased when I took the plunge. I had resigned from a well paid job with prospects. They could not know what I was attempting, it was unclear even to me. I was driven back to the Threshold of Knowing many times to rally my Self. I refused to accept that this was all there was. I wanted more and since I placed no value on my old life I was happy to throw it in the pot and see what cards I was dealt.

    Initially my euphoria kept me going but gradually as that wore off and Self doubt nibbled away I became more vulnerable to the subtle, persuasive pressure being put on me to return to the fold.

    Copies of the local paper were left open at the jobs section, discreet enquiries were made about my intentions. I was writing of course but although whilst in full time employment this was a laudable hobby as a career it was not so desirable. People would ask me, still do in fact,

    "What do you do all day long?" Let me tell you that hurts and then it makes me angry.

    At least prior to my resignation I had bought a large house to extend and renovate. This fell within understandable and acceptable parameters. I could portray my Self as an entrepreneur. Like a rat up a drain pipe, I took refuge from my exposure in the guise of a property developer whilst my thoughts gradually coalesced and my road became clearer. Camouflage.

    All the while I was feeling vulnerable and increasingly isolated. I developed an unpleasant paranoia that made me sensitive to every comment about what my job was or where I was going. I simply didn't know, I still don't. Being a solitary creature I thought I could cope. I told my Self this was the way it had to be. I became almost a recluse avoiding social situations, even going to the shops became difficult.

Eden's Legacy

My Self esteem was being undermined by my own lack of belonging and isolation. It still is, I wish I could say that identifying the problem helped, it is just something I will have to work through. Better to know what the problem is no matter how large and unpleasant, than to suffer from its symptoms in ignorance.

Whilst in the middle of my "successful" career I suffered in the same way but with the added pressure of work. No matter how busy or successful the individual the underlying conflict continues until it is engaged. What I did was remove the layer of my career that had become a dreadful distracting illusion. In my Self conscious mind I knew what I was doing at work was wrong, i.e. ignoring my responsibility to my Self and that knowledge was destroying my Self esteem and confidence. That was far worse than what I endure now.

Now I suffer less and yearn for one thing only, my own Salvation and that of Humanity. How badly or how well I perform is not so important, what matters is that I am in the right fight and going in the right direction. I am doing my best. Everything I do flows from this core belief.

We have a tendency to feel better about ourselves when we perceive ourselves as successful. This habit is tainted by our tendency to measure success in terms of material things and in comparison to how well we think others are doing. The trouble with this system is that it encourages competition, conflict. It provides no lasting comfort, we are only as good as our last victory and there are endless battles ahead.

You need to review your parameters for success, (see chap 8). This new journey cannot be measured in these material terms, they will not comfort you on the way ahead. Take this book for example for ages I was discouraged by agents and publishers, none of them were interested. For them it was about money and I allowed them to measure me and felt my Self less when they rejected me. I longed for the book signings, queues of eager publishers, the rush of being a " successful" author. I wanted to belong to all of that. It didn't happen, depression, doubt, misery. That old question came to my aid, why. Why was I writing this book?

The answer, to help make sense of my own dilemma and to aid and encourage others to do the same. I had created time and space in my life, decided what I should be doing and got on with it. Every time I sat down to think about it I came up with the same answer.

Gabriel Deeds

Some of our greatest writers have died in poverty, unrecognised by the establishment or the masses. It may be that years from now somebody will find my book and be the first person to connect with my sentiments and find solace in my words. It doesn't matter, it matters only that I have asked my Self the difficult questions and I am doing what I believe to be the right thing for me.

How on earth do you measure something like that? Well you don't. It's not the measuring on earth that counts in the long run, it's the measuring in your heart that matters and for me as a Christian the accounts are kept in Heaven. That sounds a bit glib and deep down I know that I hope to have my cake and eat it. Secretly I want the house, the boat, the life style, but I know this and don't conceal the fact. I am human but I do not deceive my Self, in this way I can control my pecuniary urges. I keep them in the open where I can see what they are up to.

How we relate to our fellow human beings is a source of immense pleasure and pain. It is completely absorbing, a life time obsession, like a complex puzzle we can't leave alone. We now recognise our own vital role in the pursuit of our personal fulfilment and Salvation. We also recognise that each of us, whilst we are unique and vital, is completely dependent on the rest of humanity.

Since few of us have the strength or the desire for total solitude, how we relate to each other, largely determines our success in achieving Enlightenment. How we treat each other, how we feel about each other, how we control our emotions, provides us with opportunity and threat. Social interaction on the level of the baboon is distracting and harmful to our objective. Social interaction on the level of a sentient, full of compassion for humanity is our greatest opportunity for advancement.

"All for one and one for all."

Resources, see also appendix 1 and 2.

Books – The History Of Mr Polly.
Movies – American Beauty, Gangs Of New York.

Chapter 13,   The body

The connection between mind and body is complex. Our moods, our frame of mind can be effected by the chemicals in our body. There are the obvious ones that we put there ourselves and there are the less obvious ones that occur naturally. As a conveyance for our Spirit, for Self, the body has many drawbacks. It is demanding and if allowed to, it can take over your life dominating every day with its needs. Treat it as you would a horse. You ride it, you are separate from it and someday you will leave it behind. It serves your purpose and you look after it in return.

    This horse is a thoroughbred. Not an easy animal to control. Just when you need it to carry you it decides to go off on its own. It is wilful and seeks to dominate you, to force you to serve it and its needs. After all that is what it is used to since you have been under the misapprehension that your body is your Self. It has many needs, some of them must be fulfilled if the horse is to survive and serve you. It must eat, drink and sleep.

    These are necessities but because they can be pleasurable the horse would like to do more eating, drinking and sleeping than is good for it. These pastimes become the reason for existence rather than a means to an end. Then there are hormones.

    This horse is a slave to it's hormones. The only thing apart from you that will distract it from eating, drinking and sleeping is another horse. Other horses to fight and to have sex with. What else is there? Oh yes, this horse is also highly strung, very emotional. It becomes angry when you try to control it and depressed if it can't get it's own way. Sometimes I think this just about sums up the Human race, no better or worse than horses.

    So here you are lumbered with this domineering, bad tempered nag that either ignores you or uses you to get what it wants. The thing is you have somewhere you have to be. To complete your journey you need to take control of the horse and train it to suit your needs.

    Above all, remember that although the relationship between you and your horse is intimate, it is not you and you are not it. You are more, you are supposed to be in charge. Although you spend every moment of your life together someday it will die. At this point how far you have travelled and in what direction will matter a great deal. So will your horse cross the finish line with you on its back to thunderous acclaim or will it have a heart attack in a massage parlour after a huge curry?

Ok, no contest, I hope, so lets take the reins and get on with it. Remember, you are the boss!

Sleep

This simple but essential need is grossly overlooked in modern society. We treat sleep as a necessary evil and cut it down to the bare minimum. At the same time we often feel that we would like more but we just cannot seem to organise it into our lives. When the alarm goes off at 7 am we find our heads stuck to the pillow. Yet at midnight the previous evening we were still going strong. You can't have it both ways.

Refer to your time management section and build sleep into your day as a priority. On average we need eight hours of sleep per day, its very simple. Buy a good bed and get in the bloody thing, eight hours a day, don't make excuses. The difference in your performance after a good nights sleep is enormous. Yes we can survive on less if we have to. In short term emergencies, when we have screwed up it, may be necessary, but for so many of us it is a way of life.

We allow ourselves to become accustomed to a lack of sleep and convince ourselves that this is a necessary life skill. How stupid. This foolishness has become embedded into the medical and nursing profession where long nights and eighty hour weeks are the norm. How implausibly ironic, how typical of the Hive that in a profession that should know better, sleep deprivation has become part of the training regime.

If for whatever reason you are not getting a good nights sleep, get your brain in gear and sort it out. There are many books on the subject and professional advice is available. Don't put up with it, don't persevere with it. If your partner is a problem consider separate beds, it's no big deal compared to not sleeping on a regular basis. Lack of sleep is a powerful weapon that the Hive will use unsparingly. Lack of sleep will make all your problems ten times worse and cripple your ability to reason and resist.

Eden's Legacy

1. Buy a good bed with particular emphasis on the mattress, take advice.
2. Make sure that you are physically and mentally tired at the right time, bedtime.
3. Get to bed eight hours before you get up.
4. Move Heaven and Earth to make sure you are not disturbed. Sleep alone if necessary.
5. Get help if you need it.

Do not underestimate what might seem a trite or simple problem.

Diet

What you put into your body via your mouth will dramatically effect how you feel and your physical and mental performance. This is not a secret, we all know this to be true, and yet once again ironically, we stuff ourselves with rubbish. To neglect your diet is to show a lack of respect for your body (your horse) and for your Self. Remember they are not the same thing. That is why so many people have a problem with their bodies. They have a problem with Self respect.

A balanced, nutritious and sufficient diet is a simple thing for us in the affluent West. By now we all know what we should be eating and how much exercise we should be getting. You don't need a fancy carbohydrate free diet, your diet is not responsible for you body, you are. If your horse is fat and ugly it is because that's the way you have been trained to see your Self. It's a huge industry, another type of conflict. A complete and very effective distraction from reality.

It is the same for alcohol and drugs although the element of escapism is greater. The vain attempt to escape our consciousness by becoming temporarily unconscious comes at a huge cost to our bodies. Such agony and incalculable suffering is accepted as the norm in our society.

It is all symptomatic of our fear of Self, our ignorance of how to begin the search for Self and a total lack of Self respect. Only you have the power to save your Self. See the appalling things that have been done to you, be aware of the conflict and your own slavery and say, "Enough"

Physical exercise

Physical exercise is a great purifier of mind and body. A long hike or a strenuous game of squash can provide release from the tension of your conflict. Balance is needed if you are to maintain your efforts over the long term. Sweat purifies and strengthens the body at the same time it distracts and relieves the mind in a positive way. Sometimes you need a change and the exacting requirements of a difficult game fit the bill. Sometimes on a long walk your mind relaxes and you will find your Self reflecting on things in a calm and very productive manner.

Explore the Martial Arts. The mental and physical discipline of the learning process is a good example and can provide much needed human contact. Your body should be sufficiently strong and healthy to aid you in your search for Self, no more no less. Gymnasiums are full of narcissistic, self centred and obsessed people who think of nothing but their next protein drink. Be careful not to allow the need to keep reasonably fit to distract you from your objective. A goal is never the objective only a step towards it.

Sex

This is where it becomes difficult to separate your Self from your body. The perceived need to reproduce or just to have sex dominates the existence of human kind. It is the very core of our biological success and perhaps the single most destructive obstacle to the discovery of Self.

We have defined the difference between Self and our bodies, the one supposedly in control of the other. We see and understand the need for control and discipline and yet it seems that all of this means little in the face of a mere chemical, testosterone or oestrogen. It is a matter of chemistry and yet the presence of these hormones can defy Self control in all of us. It obliterates common sense and rational thought and leads us straight back to our primordial past.

It seems all consuming, totally distracting, we can't get enough of it. Ultimately though it is unfulfilling and can never truly satisfy us but it can be a useful distraction for those who seek distraction. In time the fires of passion burn low and we realise that they are inconsequential, trivial but while the hormones flow they require of us determined and constant Self control.

Eden's Legacy

The mind is the most erogenous organ in the body. The stimulation of thought is where it all begins. Remember that thought is a powerful action in itself and leads to physical action. If you allow your Self to think dark thoughts even as a seemingly innocent fantasy you damage Self and may in time damage others through your actions.

For most of us sex leads to relationships and marriage but the desire for sex cannot always be contained by marriage. So we are led further into the mire of unfaithfulness, divorce and broken homes. Children without Fathers and Mothers in a stable home environment, and so the cycle of suffering continues. All because we can't keep our clothes on.

There is no easy way to deal with our desires but it is possible to master them. The question is do we want to. The answer to that has to be a resounding no. Even now we seem unable to associate cause and effect when it comes to sex and the suffering we impose on ourselves. It all comes back to awareness and whether or not you see your sexuality as a potential problem. Are you in control of it or is it in control of you.

If you see your Self and your desire as separate parts of the whole with Self in control then there is no problem. Occasionally we all slip but if you are aware of the mistake and seek to rectify it you will. If however you see desire and Self as the same thing you will behave accordingly and your desire will get you into a lot of trouble. Broken relationships, bad marriages, remote parenting, divorce, alimony, a bad reputation, even disease and death. In the final analysis you are not just an animal and behaving like one will only make you unhappy and keep you back from discovering your Self.

If you need sex in your life, and most of us do, though not all, find a loving, compatible partner who can be a friend and settle down. If you can never be satisfied by a single partner for goodness sake stay single until you can and practice safe sex. Avoid having children until you make a conscious decision to have them. Having children changes everything, and you can't send them back.

A surprising number of people are celibate for various reasons, although it is not something they would possibly talk about. Many people feel the need to lie about their sexual activity, especially young people who are often pressured into becoming sexually active too early. Often well before they know what they are doing. The consequences are devastating and remarkably, have afflicted every single generation since Adam and Eve.

Even mature adults lie about their sexual activity. If you pay any attention to surveys and polls you would be led to believe that adults have sex on average fifty seven times a week. Many is the poor fool that killed himself trying to keep up! Lots of happily married couples are sexually dormant. Surprise, surprise, there is more to life than sex.

To be celibate or abstemious is unfashionable and regarded as strange behaviour. The Hive doesn't like people to be different or independent. It also doesn't like them to be in control of their lives making conscious decisions for themselves. Celibacy, or simple abstinence, is a perfectly sensible and quite workable life option. It doesn't mean that you are "gay" or "odd" although it does mean that you will draw some fire from the Hive, if you decide to be open and forgo your right to privacy.

Marriage has traditionally been the basis of the family. A solid foundation for procreation and the raising of children. At one time it was even the only acceptable way to have sex! That's religion for you, a hot bed of hypocrisy and not very practical. Do not get married for the sake of convention or because you are frightened of being alone. You can be lonely and or miserable in a crowd, or in a marriage, that is patently obvious. Surely you don't need to experience it to find out? Forget about what other people might think or say. Unhappy marriage is a form of mass torture for our society, I haven't even mentioned God or sin, those are my personal beliefs. We suffer quite enough because of desire without even considering sin.

If you do believe in God then your actions are strictly governed by those beliefs, period. Live your life accordingly and you will find peace, contradict your own beliefs and you will suffer. It is perfectly simple.

Your body is the vehicle for your consciousness until we can manage to do without it. Respect your Self and respect your body.

Resources, see also appendix 1 and 2.

Books – Desperately Seeking Snoozin. (John Wiedman)

Chapter 14 The mind

Emotion

"Nothing appeals more strongly to the irrational, emotional side of us than religion. Humans are more readily motivated by emotion than by reason."

Diane M. Walton

  Emotion gets in the way of reality. When we are emotional we say and do things that we do not mean, and yet these words and deeds have consequences. Very often when we display emotion it evokes emotion in others who act in turn without thought. The spiral into chaos and suffering is plain to see all around our world.

  Emotion is a hangover from our primal roots when intelligence was minimal and responses to certain situations were regulated by chemical stimuli. When we are frightened or threatened we produce adrenaline in the fight or flight response. We then run away or we become angry and fight, violence leads to hatred and hatred leads to violence. We win or we lose in the perpetual conflict of survival.

  Then comes Desire, the need to reproduce, the desire to mate. Love, lust and jealousy lead to fear, anger and hatred. All of our emotions are deeply rooted in the evolutionary cycle, they are as potent today as ever. The chemicals that course through our veins override conscious thought and determine our actions. We are pre-programmed like robots by nature's alchemy. None of us are immune to its power, but we can be aware of it, we can control it.

  In the Meditation on the Bodies, we allowed ourselves to experience emotions and tried to determine what was driving them before walking away from them. Reflection, meditation, is the antidote for emotion. Reflection requires time and space, both deadly to emotion. Before emotion strikes or after it has cooled, take the time to analyse your emotional feelings. Untangle the knot and follow the thread to the underlying root cause.

Gabriel Deeds

Emotions always obscure the truth and always lead to suffering. They are always symptomatic of something else and like any good physician you need to treat the cause not the effect.

Love

So how can a good emotion like love lead to suffering? Is love an emotion? Well if you are talking about God's love for Humanity, even that, pure as it is, causes suffering, to God. However that suffering has purpose since He intends for us to be reclaimed. Is that love an emotion? No, it is much more than that. If you are talking about love between a man and a woman, now there is real emotion and real suffering. Partly because the definition of love gets screwed up by biology, desire, and loneliness and partly because we have no idea what it is anyway. For the most part this suffering has no purpose and serves only to perpetuate the cycle of emotion and suffering.

We transfer all the vague unease and unhappiness of an unfulfilled, directionless, existence into the search for love. It may as well be the moon. We search for that special person who will give our existence meaning and make life bearable. How many people do you know who have found this kind of love from a relationship? How many people do you know who have been to Hell and back over their relationships?

It is not impossible to find true love in this way, just bloody unlikely. How many people do you know who have achieved a kind of acceptable, comfortable habit in their relationships? How many of us simply live in stasis, limbo, submerged in the myriad details of relationship, family and career? Is this love? It can certainly generate emotion, lots of it, but love it ain't.

This kind of love is ephemeral, transient like the difference between happiness and peace. There is a huge difference between our corrupted definition of love and true compassion.

Compassion is what we need, love is what we want.

True love is not an emotion, but it can cause us to be emotional. The love of a Mother for her child is ever present. Even when she is asleep she loves her child. It is above passion and emotion. If the child is threatened, then you will see emotion, driven by adrenaline, not love.

Eden's Legacy

She will defend her child, but so would any Mother in the animal kingdom.

The difference is true love, not emotion. A human Mother can love her child until the day she dies and even, perhaps, beyond. A baboon will wean her baby and move on to have another. There are uncomfortable parallels, for not all humans are sentient, but true love goes beyond emotion, beyond desire, beyond biology.

Ask a Mother to compare her love for her husband to the love of her children. Then we begin to define the true nature of love. Taken a step further, how will that Mother react in a situation where a stranger's child is threatened? She is able to love all children because she has an affinity with her child, all children, with all Mothers and all women.

She has known love and suffering, she shares that bond with all Mothers and all children.

Truly, if the world were run by women, we would be a lot better off. This is as near as I can get to describing real love, but even this must go further. For true love must extend to all. A truly daunting aspiration, one that we can boggle at dumfounded.

There is hope however. Just as a Mother develops the ability to experience a broader love, a kind of sisterhood, so men can experience it in the unlikely setting of war. They come to feel a bond with their comrades, brothers at arms. The men who have shared their suffering and helped each other to survive it.

Ask any old war horse why they suffered as they did and they will tell you. It was not for Queen or country, honour or glory but for their comrades. It was for the guy lying in the mud beside him, half starved, terrified and yet closer than a lover. (All Quiet On The Western Front, appendix 2)

The next step is the remarkable realisation that he has more in common with the men in the line opposite, the enemy, than he does with patriotism or honour or glory. The most notable example of this occurred in the First World War, at Christmas. The troops, enjoying an unofficial cease fire, sang Christmas carols and shared their meagre rations. They even played football together.

The High command quickly intervened with courts martial and transfer of the units involved to other sectors. Both the British and the

Gabriel Deeds

German High commands reacted in the same way. Terrified their troops would not fight, terrified someone would ask the dread question,
"Why!"
Through the concentrated, shared, futile suffering that is the cost of war, men begin to realise the folly of it all and would have stopped it. There masters who lacked the wisdom of their experience drove them on until one side could "win". When they returned home they were lost, unable to cope with their new awareness. Unable to share their knowledge with anyone who had not experienced it. This concentrated, shared suffering accelerates the process of Enlightenment. On their return to the "real" world they are bereft. Separated from their comrades and surrounded by shallow, obvious illusion. They are out of step, changed forever.

So it is we all can experience unconditional love and Enlightenment through the shared bonds of suffering. Having experienced it and become aware of it so we are empowered to love not just ourselves but all of humanity. True love is revealed to us and its name is compassion.

"For God so loved the world that he gave his only son"

"Greater love hath no man than he lay down his life for another"

Just as all Mothers and children are united by love so all of humanity is united by God's love, the Universal Consciousness' love, and by our own suffering. Until we become aware of this love for us we share the common chains of suffering. When we become aware of this love so we finally see all of humanity in the light of compassion and shared suffering.

No one is excluded.

Emotion is illusion and leads to suffering just as sure as night follows day. It seems however that we are not soon parted from it, so we have to learn to live with it. Treat it as you would a poisonous reptile. Avoid it if you can, or handle it with care as you scrutinise it. You cannot think and be emotional, the two are diametrically opposed, each a different system for coping with life. One is for animals and one is for sentient people. We used to be mere animals, we can be more. The transition is long and difficult. The boundaries between thought and emotion overlap and blur, they coexist within us, uncomfortably.

Buddhists are often accused of being cold. In fact it is merely that they have made the distinction between emotion and the Self and spend much time and effort controlling emotion. Their resulting calmness can be perceived as coolness or even coldness and sets them apart. In fact they may be full of peace and equanimity but at the same time aware of how difficult it is to maintain and how careful they need to be.

Thought

"I think therefore I am." My thoughts are generated by me, but they are not me, they are of me. Just as light comes from the sun but is not the sun.

Separating your Self or your soul from your physical body is a concept we are familiar with. Separating your Self from your mind is a lot more difficult since we tend to regard our minds, our intellect, as the essence of humanity. Understandable since it differentiates us from all other known species, we are proud of it, we know that it is real.

We accept its existence without question even though it is intangible. We experience it within ourselves and we see the results of it in art, literature and science. If we think about it though, the mind is another layer to be peeled away as we begin to discover Self. Its existence is evidence of, something else, something bigger, deeper. It is proof that the inner core that is mysterious, elusive and so disturbing actually exists. (Meditation on the bodies, chapter 9)

Our species could never leave such a mystery alone. Our natural curiosity and Spirituality will take us there sooner or later, regardless of belief. In time, Self or the Soul, whatever you want to call it, will be better understood. It will be accepted as we accept our bodies and our minds. The further we travel from our primal roots the closer we get to being comfortable with Self and all the things not yet even conceived outside the current puny cycle of our existence.

There is nowhere else for us to go. It is inevitable.

Within this unexplored Universe is the Spiritual connection, the spark of Divinity into which Self begins to merge and lose much of its significance. The drop falls into the ocean and is not lost but becomes a part of something else, the cosmic sea. Within its cool depths is found Enlightenment, peace. The next level, and the next and the next without limit or constraint into infinity.

Our daily thoughts are mostly incredibly mundane compared to the feeling or sensation of being a part of the cosmic sea. Power, ambition, health, wealth and happiness, pale into insignificance as trivial as a sex kitten's pedicure. They can logically be divided into those thoughts that fall within the Higher mind and those that fall within the lower mind. The trail runs from the physical body to the lower mind and the emotions. It then runs from lower to Higher mind and from Higher mind to Self and from Self to who knows where. I believe that it leads to a Universal Consciousness but I also believe that the term Universal Consciousness means many things. I won't know until I get there and I can't get there on my own.

Some of our thoughts however, especially those connected to our emotions are very dark indeed. Have you ever contemplated killing someone or robbing a bank or illicit sex with someone completely beyond the pale?

The difference between thought and action is just sufficient to keep us out of jail. A thought may seem harmless in the privacy of your own mind, not so. A harmless thought turns into a fantasy which can ultimately become physical action. You may feel secure in the knowledge that whatever you think is private, secret from every person who might be offended, hurt or even destroyed by what you are thinking.

This illusion of secrecy corrupts our thoughts and actions. To use the driving analogy again, we feel anonymous in the privacy and controlled environment of our cars. We are detached from personal contact and social responsibility and our actions can sometimes be deplorable. We can abuse another driver without fear of embarrassment or retaliation. As soon as that driver becomes a person our behaviour changes dramatically.

We modify our behaviour because we know the difference between right and wrong and because we have to live together. Our actions have real consequences. Anti social behaviour, brawling with another motorist can also end in police intervention. Hypocrisy? Maybe, but without these control mechanisms our physical lives would be impossibly chaotic. Within our minds there are no rights and wrongs. We can think what we like and seem to hurt no one. There is little or no control and so we live in chaos and suffering.

The illusion of privacy in our thoughts causes us to think in a chaotic and unrestrained fashion. Many of us think that this is all right that free thought is a bastion of civilisation. It is, but it carries responsibility. It can be unrestrained, without fear of consequence, unfettered by any control mechanism, but there are consequences.

Thought is power and power is nothing without control. What you are in essence, is reflected by your thoughts, these thoughts can damage or promote Self. You cannot find and understand your Self until you have understood the nature and purpose of thought. The outward manifestation of your Self is based on what you think. Your actions demonstrate your thought or lack of it. Bad thoughts bring suffering.

"Those who live in accordance with these divine laws without complaining, firmly established in faith, are released from karma. Those who violate these laws, criticizing and complaining, are utterly deluded, and are the cause of their own suffering."

The Bhagavad Gita 3:31-32

The sad fact is that in general we exercise precious little control over our thinking process at all. We don't think about thinking, its something we do mostly on a superficial level. Why?

There is no obvious quality control on our thoughts, no thought police. Nobody knows what we are thinking, remember. We are anonymous, seemingly free from consequences and responsibility for our thoughts. There is no teacher to force us to use the power of thought wisely. It's a bit like going to college for the first time straight from school. At school the teachers kept tight control over your work, things are different at college. The work is still there for you to do but now you are a responsible adult, you are expected to supervise your Self. Some do, some don't, but there is always the threat of the final exam.

We think and therefore live as if there was no final exam. The consequences are chaos and misery, but are your thoughts entirely anonymous, completely secret? No they are not. I believe that God knows what you are thinking, but regardless of whether or not you believe in God, you know what you are thinking.

What mechanism then can control our thoughts? There are two.

1. Self control, you are responsible for your Self and your thoughts.
2. Religion.

Self control (Thought)

You know what your innermost secret thoughts are. If you have racist thoughts, no matter how deep and private, you are a racist. This is a basic truth. However that doesn't mean that you will admit it to your Self. Don't go off at a tangent here racism is a mere example. Consider the fact that your actions are what you think, this is fundamental.

Lets stick with racism for now, there are many far worse examples, but we are not ready for those yet. Remember your thoughts are private from the rest of the world, don't be frightened to think them honestly at this point. If you can't even be honest with your Self what is the point of anything?

I am a racist. I know I am. At first I scoffed at the notion but I have caught myself on occasion encouraged by the press to think ill of my fellow human beings who just happen to be a different colour. I qualified this with the justification that as immigrants to my country these individuals made no attempt to integrate with my cultures and beliefs, that they were hostile to me. I argued that they were abusing the system and soaking up resources, taking work and housing that I and my kind could use. They were a bad influence with their gangs and drugs and crime. They had wrecked their own countries and now they would wreck mine. True or false, it doesn't matter.

I realised that they were different and I saw them as a threat and so I discriminated against them as the Hive has taught us to do. They will win or I will win, conflict, survival of the fittest. This of course is all in my mind however, because racism is deeply unfashionable at the moment, depending on where you live that is. This civilised veneer is microns thick and the fertile seed bed of racism lies beneath. Look around you. Remember again, this is not a question of whether or not you are a racist but a question of the process of thought involved in examining the situation.

Eden's Legacy

We travel swiftly from denial to justification in a very adversarial way even within our own minds we tend to try and justify ourselves or even deceive ourselves completely. This is the danger, Self deceit and illusion, hypocrisy and dishonesty. A good old fashioned red neck can be educated and cured of what is essentially ignorance. (The Defiant Ones, appendix 2) However, an educated person who is able to deceive themselves, is far worse. Externally that person could be the Human Resources director for the United Nations, a stalwart defender of human rights but when their daughter brings home a boyfriend of a different colour? The truth is within you, seek it out.

Relax in the privacy of your thoughts, you are not going to get anywhere except into trouble deceiving your Self. Firstly accept the possibility that you are racist, it's not uncommon, just unfashionable. Forget the fact that at present it is a trait that exhibited openly will get you attacked in every quarter, this is a private debate. Nobody has the right or the ability to invade your thoughts, you have a responsibility to have them freely and examine them objectively. How can you tackle serious issues if you are unwillingly to examine them even in your own mind?

I accept that I am basically a racist. There, now I can take the next step, why am I racist? People naturally discriminate, it's how we pigeonhole our fellow humans. There are those within our family, tribe, community, society, we discriminate against them too in different ways to different degrees. Then there are those outside of all of these categories. We tend to view these outsiders as inferior competitors and we guard our sense of belonging jealously. If we are threatened economically and jobs or housing are involved this tends to magnify the effect. This is human nature and something that we all have in common, regardless of race or creed, we are all children of the Hive.

Since I understand my racism I can perceive it for what it is, ignorance and conditioning, a hangover from our primordial past. I can spot it and discount it as nonsense because I have thought it through.

So if you truly examine your thoughts, honestly and systematically, you can draw the poison and heal the wounds of your life's experience. Honestly seeking and confronting your demons is the only way to move forward.

Gabriel Deeds

Religion.

Even habitual religion and the associated guilt it confers is of some use in controlling and regulating thought. At least it gives us some kind of starting point and a familiarity with the concept of thinking "Good" and "Bad" thoughts and the consequences thereof. The millions of us who have not been exposed to even rudimentary religion and morality, have only the eager embrace of the Hive to give life the illusion of meaning. This is a truly depressing place for anyone to start from.

I was brought up with habitual religion and walked away from it. It was only years later that I was able to make sense of what I had been remorselessly exposed to as a child. It was then that I became aware of the difference between religion and Spirituality and was able to separate the two. I revisited the teachings of Christ without cynicism and bitterness and was inspired and comforted.

Thought is the powerhouse of everything of any consequence in our lives. Every action, everything we say or do comes from our thought process. The quality of the end product is directly proportional to how much thought we invest. Serious thought brings us ultimately to Spirituality which in turn affects all of our actions. Most of what we do in our lives is of no moment, it has no meaning because we give our lives so little thought, why is that?

It is because we know subconsciously that a hidden Self exists. Yet we fail to acknowledge it in our lives, we fear it. It goes against our Hive conditioning which is nothing more than animal instinct. It also seems such a huge task, we don't know where to start, how can we as individuals be so important? Well we are, you are, and it is a huge task, remember it is nothing less than your life's work!

As your awareness grows your thoughts will grow in intensity and meaning. They will graduate away from the mundane to the profound. Gradually day by day, your awareness will grow until every day, every action and every thought will be a part of your overall objective of personal discovery and fulfilment. It's a long journey.

Defence – conclusion

These are the main defensive weapons that I have in my armoury, remember to use them. That may seem like a strange thing to say but as I write to you about them I realise that I have not used them enough. Learn to use them, add to them and practice systematically as the Hive has taught you. Be proactive, do not simply read and file this information, that is not enough. Years, perhaps decades of inertia must be swept aside, hence the action plan in chapter 15. Read and re-read this book and others you find, practice, practice, practice. When you are embroiled in the day to day struggle, Spiritual and physical, it is easy to become lost in the details. Vigilance is essential, but it is not always enough.

Your primary defence is your awareness of your struggle for Self. Imagine that you are a defector. For years you were a part of the machine that suppressed and crushed the people. Finally you realised your mistake and gradually, little by little became an agent of C.H.A.N.G.E., a secret underground organisation. Your activities were noticed by the Hive and now you languish in an interrogation suite, waiting. Your interrogators have no scruples, they know you, literally, as well as you know your Self. They are ruthless and they are remorseless.

You, however, are well trained in counter interrogation techniques having read this book and practiced its techniques. You know what they will try to do, you understand what they are about. You are strong. All their mind games and tricks will fail because, ultimately, they can only win if you allow them to. You have no secrets from them, their childish game is futile. They cannot hurt you, you can only hurt your Self. You are aware.

It is only when you become aware of your condition that you will be able to motivate and organise your Self to begin the job that will give your life meaning and direction, inner peace and contentment.

If you have a clear objective and solid goals to achieve that objective, any suffering you endure will be for a purpose. It will be a sign of progress, it is part of your new existence as a more Enlightened, sentient being.

The next and final chapter will help you maintain momentum and utilise your practical skills learned at the feet of the Hive. We will use them to formulate a plan of action uniquely tailored to your needs. This plan represents a refining process that will never end. It will become a part of your life and a means of targeting and measuring your efforts to best effect.

Remember action plans are a Hive tool designed to increase efficiency and productivity. We are using Hive tactics for our own personal objectives, not to become more effective slaves. Don't be led astray by the Hive, use its own power against it. Keep Eden's Legacy handy a re-read it at regular intervals. Don't leave it to chance, you will forget, you will be distracted. Aim to read it every month!

As you progress, so will your plan. It will be a constant guide to be updated and modified at regular intervals throughout your life. As time goes by you will become more Enlightened and more aware of how much you have to learn, how much damage you need to repair.

Before we begin the "doing" bit, take a moment to celebrate your Self. Hopefully something has changed within you. Not obviously, not dramatically but in the only way that really matters, deep within your Self. Being is more important than doing, create the fertile garden of equanimity, time and space, within your Self and everything else will follow.

Resources, see also appendix 1 and 2.

Books – Destructive emotions, the Dalai Lama.
Movies – Matrix, All Quiet On The Western Front.

Chapter 15   The Action Plan

I have a drawer full of action plans, I don't think I ever read one of them. I am sure we are all familiar with those courses, team building, motivation, communications, you know the ones I mean. We come back from a course full of what we have learned and two days later we are back to our old habits.

Try using your work to help you with your action plan, especially with the assessment side. Your boss may be a valuable resource and may even help with courses and training. Convince her that you are worth the investment, because you are. If you have a regular work appraisal that might be a good way of monitoring your performance in your own action plan. If you are not systematically appraised, ask to be. That is sure to impress and will be useful to you personally.

Well action plans aren't for everyone, but don't be too cynical. It is very easy to be negative and sneer but if you want things to change you need a little Self discipline. You need to use all the help you can get. Just because we use and abuse the ubiquitous action plan does not mean that it cannot be a useful tool. The biggest problem with the search for Self is that so much of it is non specific and intangible. We struggle to get a handle on it, we don't know what to do next so we don't do anything. Hence the action plan, so bear with it.

A word of warning, it is important that we make a clear distinction between objectives and goals. The objective is the end product, the goals are designed to create that product. Some people use the terms the other way around, fine, as long as you know the difference between them.

Do not get hung up on goals, they are a means to and end i.e. the objective. It is very easy to get caught up in achieving a goal that we perhaps enjoy or find easier than others. Remember that the action plan is not designed to be followed slavishly. Be prepared to modify and adapt it where necessary. It is designed to access and augment your intelligence and logic faculties, not to replace them. When we have a plan we can tap into the tide of human dynamism that once activated and directed is so powerful.

Gabriel Deeds

Be very careful when setting your goals. You can end up with far too many. Look for root causes of problems. For example you might be constantly short of time when in fact you are short of Self discipline. Make Self discipline your goal and good time management a measure of success. We will go through our goals very carefully in a moment, but first our objective.

Objective

A clear, strong objective is absolutely imperative to the successful conclusion of any enterprise. Without one you will never achieve anything except confusion. It is astonishing how often we begin major projects as a species or individually without a simple objective, especially in the corporate world. For me the objective is simple, personal Salvation or put another way, Enlightenment. This inevitably flows from my beliefs.

1. I believe in the Universal Consciousness. I call this power God as a Christian.
2. I believe that I am a part of the Universal Consciousness and that it is part of me.
3. I believe that I am responsible for my own Salvation and that this is my objective.
4. I believe that Self sacrifice, helping others, is my route to Salvation.
5. I believe that I must live as my beliefs dictate.

It is immediately obvious that everyone is eventually going to have their own beliefs. I am fortunate and unusual in that I have clear beliefs and an objective. Most people do not. At this point you have several confusing choices.

1. You can spend as much time as it takes to establish your beliefs, see chapter 7 and so set your objective. This could take years.
2. You can use my objective and modify things as you progress.
3. You can use your current beliefs to set an objective and modify things as you progress.

4. For those with no religious or Spiritual beliefs your objective could be to maximise your personal potential and modify things as you progress.

It is important that our objective is simple and clear. It is my intention to provide you with a template that can be modified if necessary and yet we are all different so this is very difficult. I feel that option 4 is best suited to our needs in this instance, Self is the common factor in all of this. Your objective will therefore be,
To seek personal fulfilment. This is not as vague as it may sound. We will get to specifics when we start to examine goals. If you manage to establish your beliefs in the future you might want to modify your objective to make it more specific. For now you need to start somewhere.

Goals

There are some important rules to remember when setting goals.

Goal setting
1. All goals must clearly work towards achieving your objective.
2. A goal must never be confused with the objective.
3. All goals must be specific, clear and simple. Don't have too many.
4. All goals must be measurable in some way.
5. All goals must be monitored and reviewed systematically.

Goal setting can now begin. There are some that I regard as essential and some that you will need to determine for your Self.

Gabriel Deeds

Action Plan

Objective – Personal fulfilment
Goal 1 – Time and space, the fertile garden. (Chapters 9/10)

Time management

Organise a course through work or online and read the recommended books, (appendix 1). Set a completion deadline and review your performance. Ask your boss, family and friends to assess you and determine which aspects of your time management need to go into next years plan. (See chap 9/10 for resources).

Meditation

Begin an ongoing program of meditation as suggested and read the recommended books. Set a completion deadline for basic and intermediate meditation. Your teacher will help you with targets and assessment. Meditation is a long term form of time management and need not involve religion. (See chap 9/10 for resources, and appendix 1)

Assertion skills

Again, organise a course, study the recommended reading and set completion deadlines. Ask your boss, family and friends to assess your performance. Review your progress and determine those elements of assertion you need to work on. Repeat the process in next years plan. (See chap 10). Pick a difficult situation with a problem person and resolve it with your new skills.

Goal 2 – Establish your beliefs, sow the seeds (chapter 7)

Review your historical beliefs with an open mind. Study the literature of your own beliefs, talk to your local Priest, Imam, Monk. Set a deadline for completion, review and assess your beliefs. Write them down in black and white.

Study and compare

Check out other philosophies and teachings. Go to a Mosque, Church etc, meet people of other faiths, talk to them.

Eden's Legacy

Establish your belief

Choose a moral code to live by. It doesn't have to be religious, demonstrate your belief. Learn the code and measure your Self in thought word and deed.

Goal 3 – Live your life accordingly, tend your crops

Analyse

Analyse your personal strengths and weaknesses as per the personal profile and SWOT analysis.

Identify

Identify the things you need to change, (weeding). Ask your boss, your friends and family. Explain and ask them to be honest, be honest with your Self.

Implement

Implement measurable strategies to improve your Self, (see examples further on).

Goals 1 and 2 are self explanatory, and they will help immensely with goal 3. Goal 3 requires a little Self examination. Goal 3 is the one that is unique to you and you are the only one who can determine what needs to be done. The following exercises will help you to analyse your own personality traits, good and bad. We can then accentuate the positive and eliminate the negative, or try to.

Remember the lists you prepared earlier, now is the time to use them. First you should list your own strengths and weaknesses as you perceive them. This is surprisingly difficult. It's all too easy when we are talking about someone else. Let us turn this unfortunate human trait to our advantage.

Think of people you admire, ask your Self why you admire them? Think of people you dislike, why do you dislike them? There are a few categories over the page to get you started. Add your own, be honest, ask those who know you the best. Just hand them the score sheet below and, without recrimination, add up the points. Explain that you are

Gabriel Deeds

trying to improve your Self and be a better person. This is an uncomfortable thing to do but it is also a positive and necessary thing to do.

Most people will be surprised to be invited to tell you what they really think of you. When they understand why you are doing this they will admire you for it and generally you will find that their feedback will be helpful. Follow up and ask them to clarify points that they have made. When they see that you are serious and not going to get mad they will open up even further. Treat them as a resource to aid you in setting your personal goals and attaining them.

Make it clear that you do not want overt negative criticism but positive criticism which you can use. Be choosy about who you ask but don't avoid people who may be uncomfortably honest. Thank them for their help and if you decide to use their feedback tell them. Ask them if it would be possible for you to come back after a given period and ask if they have detected any improvement.

When receiving feedback it is important that you do not react negatively. You have asked for an opinion and received one. These people are trying to help you. If you honestly feel that they are being unfair, discount their opinions. If more than one person says the same thing you will have to face facts. For the most part they will be telling you what you already know, now is the time to accept your flaws and deal with them.

> If you can trust your Self,
> When all men doubt you,
> And yet take account of their
> doubting too.

From "If", by Rudyard Kipling, see appendix 1.

Eden's Legacy

Personal strengths and weakness' score sheet

Weakness   **Strength**

1   2   3   4   5   6   7   8   9   10

Loyal
Faithful
Honest
Generous
Patient
Determined
Assertive
Outspoken
Independent
Optimistic
Good listener
Organised
Affectionate
Open
Communication
Temper
Sense of humour
Extrovert
Introvert
Team player
Loner
Creative
Self disciplined
Consistent

Anything below 6 needs work

Gabriel Deeds

By now you should have a pretty good idea of the personality traits that need work. You probably haven't learned anything you didn't already know but it is useful to emphasise and highlight potential goals for your action plan. Take some time to summarise the traits that you have identified before completing the next exercise.

Remember the lists that you produced, regrets page 29, the things you are dishonest about page 95, the things you dislike about your life page 131. Lots of material here.

Personality profile

Another useful tool to help us in this process is a basic personality profile to identify your strengths and weaknesses. It takes about five minutes online to answer four questions about your personality. You may be surprised at how accurate the test is. After the test you will be told which category you belong to. Remember it is a generalisation but it will give you some useful pointers to start you off. It's also great fun.

www.haleonline.com/psychtest/

When you have established which category you belong to go the site below for a more in depth analysis of your personality traits.

www.typelogic.com

I find it amazing how insightful these tests are. No matter how alone or isolated you feel there are millions of others suffering as you do. The summary of your personality traits includes potential weaknesses, add them to your list. At this stage you should have more than enough material, now we need to begin refining it. The next exercise is designed to do just that. We need to reduce all this data to bite sized chunks that we can turn into achievable, measurable goals.

SWOT Analysis

SWOT Analysis is a very effective way of identifying your Strengths and Weaknesses, and of examining the Opportunities and Threats you face. Carrying out an analysis using the SWOT framework helps you to set specific and clear goals for your action plan.

Strengths

What are your advantages?
What do you do well?
What relevant resources do you have?
What do other people see as your strengths?

Consider this from your own point of view and from the point of view of the people around you. Don't be modest. Be realistic. If you are having any difficulty with this, try writing down a list of your characteristics. Some of these will hopefully be strengths and some will be weaknesses. Can you foresee any of these strengths becoming opportunities? How?

Weaknesses

What could you improve?
What do you do badly?
What should you avoid?

Again, consider this from an internal and external basis: Do other people perceive weaknesses that you do not see? Can you foresee any of these weaknesses becoming a threat? Are they holding you back?

Opportunities

Where are the good opportunities facing you?
What interesting things are happening to you?

A useful approach to looking at opportunities is to look at your strengths and ask your Self whether these open up any opportunities. Alternatively, look at your weaknesses and ask your Self whether you could open up opportunities by eliminating them.

Gabriel Deeds

Threats

What obstacles do you face?
Could any of your weaknesses be threats?

Carrying out this analysis will often be illuminating both in terms of pointing out what needs to be done, and in putting problems into perspective.

Take all the above and place them in the matrix below. Try not to duplicate. The matrix contains my data to give you the idea.

Swot Analysis

Strength	Weakness
Independent	Lacks Self confidence
Strong willed	Poor social skills
Used to change	Self discipline
Intelligent	Time management
Educated	Volatile temperament
Honest	Communication
Aware	Stubborn
Self motivated	Assertion
Family	
Faith	
Enough money	

Opportunity	Threat
Personal Salvation	Unclear goals
Fulfilment	Isolation
Change	Self doubt
Learn new skills	Poor communication
New career	Tired
Meet new people	Lonely
	Self discipline
	Money

From all of this we need to extract only two personal goals to work on. Remember it is important to keep it simple, achievable and measurable. Goal one, time management, meditation and assertion will prove invaluable in meeting your personal goals. That's why they are mandatory. Some of my weaknesses and threats are already covered in goal one. For example Self discipline, time management and volatility are extensively covered in the practice of meditation. It also helps in creating an interesting and enjoyable social experience which makes me less isolated and lonely. Whilst striving to learn to assert my Self it is also necessary for me to improve my communication skills.

In this way, by killing as many birds as possible with one stone, it is possible to whittle down the list to make it more manageable. Some of the things on your list may well be useful in measuring your performance. For example in my meditation I will concentrate on emotion such as anger and attempt to understand what causes it. This understanding is a measure of success in both meditation and anger management. It is necessary to be creative in measuring performance.

Completion of a workshop on Self esteem is a measure of success and will in turn lead to possible ways to improve the situation. It is important that the process is controlled, measured and systematically reviewed. It can become very convoluted and you may find your Self getting side tracked or confused. If you stick to the process this will become apparent and can be dealt with.

Now we need to take all this information on your personality and turn it into something simple and specific. Remember we do not want too many goals or sub goals. changing any aspect of your personality is difficult so select only two initially. Consider every point that was raised and reflect on each. Consider that there may be patterns or common themes connecting problem areas. For example people who feel threatened or afraid are often bad tempered and irritable. They may be shy, even anti social but is important to realise the difference between root causes and symptomatic behaviour. You should set goals designed to deal with causes, not symptoms. In this case you should try and identify the source of fear and deal with it.

In my own example the root cause was low Self esteem. It was only after I was told by those who knew me that I realised I was being aggressive and irritable. It was only after counselling that I realised that low Self esteem was the problem and was able to address the issue. One thing leads to another and your goals may need to be modified as you become more aware of your problems. Another good reason for keeping the number of goals manageable.

Eden's Legacy

My initial goal was to deal with my anger. I did this in a measurable way by seeing a councillor and so discovered my low Self esteem. The new goal therefore became understanding my low Self esteem and improving it. This led to a course, through my work and some cognitive therapy, in short some useful tips to modify my thinking and behaviour.

List all of your personality traits in the matrix and then look for those common denominators and patterns. These and your own intelligence will lead you to your personal goals.

The Hive has only a few templates to use on us. It is very predictable once you understand how it works. Since it cannot reason or think it relies on regimented behavioural control to enslave us. This means that no matter how unique we are as individuals the type of suffering we endure is something that we can share with our fellow victims. It is something that unites us all in a common bond. If we can but realise this, become aware of it, it becomes a source of profound strength and comfort.

Identify the wounds inflicted on you and how they make you behave badly. Anger, intolerance and hate all tend to emphasise and renew the cycle of suffering. Once you face them and find the courage to seek help from others you will find that they too suffer as you do. You will realise that together you have the power to vanquish the Hive and assume the responsibility for your own destiny. Individually and collectively we can move on in our evolution We can break out of this primal repeating loop, this vicious circle in which we have been trapped for so long. We can finally move to the next level and beyond.

Chapter 16   Conclusion

As in all cycles, the end is merely the prelude to a new beginning. Wherever you find your Self in your own cycle of life, remember that you are a fundamental player in the overall cycle of existence. You are connected to the Universal Consciousness, a drop in the cosmic sea. You are what it is constructed of, a brick in the wall. That brick must be good and strong or the wall will be weak.

You can build nothing until you have made your Self aware of your flaws and the damage that has been done to you. Until you have honestly tackled the repair work and striven to take your place in the foundation. Until you have realised you're true worth and directed your life's force towards personal fulfilment.

Your life, you, are a rare and precious thing. An opportunity for the advancement of your Self and of all creation. This opportunity carries with it a heavy responsibility. You and you alone are responsible for the fulfilment of your own potential. There are benign forces that will help, but none that will take away the burden that is Eden's Legacy. Only you have the power to save your Self.

The truth of all of this has been obscured and twisted by those generations that have preceded you and by your own primal instincts and fears. Your predecessors have collectively failed you, victims of their own fear and ignorance. Not only have they failed you, they have attacked and violated you from childhood, to perpetuate the Hell that they have constructed. They have failed to understand and control their fear. They have failed to act against the tyranny of the Hive preferring what they know, no matter how vile, no matter that it is pain and suffering. As a result we live in a vale of tears.

Every culture has its legends of a Messiah. One who will come and take away the pain and suffering that we inflict daily on ourselves and each other. We wait and wait and wait, sometimes for generations, millennia even, for someone to come and take away our own birthright. The responsibility that we alone bear, metaphorically stolen from the tree of Knowledge in the Garden of Eden, the knowledge of Good and Evil. That knowledge brings with it the crushing burden of choice. You must pick a side. Then, having chosen, every moment of your existence, every thought and act must be governed by your beliefs.

No one will come to save you, you must save your Self.

It falls to you then, to understand and to become aware of the conflict and what it has done to you. To choose your side and to fight. There is no abstention, no fence to sit on, to do so is in itself a choice, the wrong choice.

"For Evil to flourish all that is needed is for good people to do nothing."

Sooner or later the conflict will reach you, it will come for you and yours. We are like Hobbits, living our busy lives in suburbia whilst others fight our fight for us. You can suffer as an insignificant slave until you can endure no more, or you can step up to the breach and take your place. Yes you will suffer, but you suffer now. Give your life and your suffering meaning. Establish your beliefs, set your objective and goals, roll up your sleeves and begin. Regardless of what you decide you believe, peace will find you somewhere along the way.

I have tried my best to move you with words. To stimulate your mind and to spur your thoughts to action. I have even suggested a course of action to help you break the inertia that plagues our lives. Books to read, movies to watch, courses to organise and attend.

Now, it is your turn. Now, having read this book, you cannot say that you were never told, that you did not know. I have reminded you of the truth that dwells within, buried deep. The knowledge of what is right and what is wrong and the perpetual struggle between the two. This is Eden's Legacy, choice, responsibility.

Now that the book is finished, "reality" will kick in. All that was raised and discussed will fall away into silence, if you let it. All the most reasonable explanations for inaction will rise up like summer weeds to prevail upon you to do, nothing. It's too late, too hard, too unrealistic compared to your busy life. It is so much easier to drop the book onto the bed and let it slip to the floor, to slide quietly underneath with the dark and the dust. The Hive stands poised, like a burglar in your bedroom, you stir in your sleep and it freezes, desperate for you to return to your slumbers.

Gabriel Deeds

The words in this book are written in your heart, an echo of the Truth you already know. You cannot hide from reality indefinitely, and remember, you do not have all the time in the world.

No book can do it for you, only you have the power and the responsibility that is Eden's Legacy. As you turn this last page on our short journey together the Universe waits with baited breath. Full of hope, it watches closely to see what you will do. To see whether you will decide to be a slave or a warrior?

The only way to a better future, is to build it your Self.

PTO

Epilogue

Some day all the lights will come on at the same time and the Universe will be filled with the light of compassion and Enlightenment. Until then however we must all do our best to raise our own level of awareness and to influence as many people as we can. If you know of anyone who may find these words inspiring or comforting, please spread the word.

Ask your local library for the book, if they haven't got one ask if they will get it for you. Lend or give your book, buy spare copies as gifts, email details of the book and the website to your friends.

www.edenslegacy.com

Start with the list you made in chapter 12, all the people you love. Speculate, try it on people that perhaps you would hesitate to talk to about such things. Talking about the book will break down barriers in surprising places. To hell with small talk, stick your neck out a little. Throw your pebble into the cosmic sea and make a few ripples. A few ripples can become a wave.

All the lights will all come on some day, lets see if we can make it sooner rather than later. May your God, the Universal consciousness, go with you.

Gabriel Deeds.

Appendix 1   Recommended reading and Web sites.

Religion

The Koran
The Koran (Penguin) by NJ Dawood.
The Holy Quaran by Alamah Nooruddin.
The Qur'an Translation by Abdullah Yusuf Ali.
Understanding Islam by Thomas Lippman.
The Bible
The New International Version (NIV), also on audio.
Introducing The New Testament by William Drane.
The agony by Elizabeth White.
The Bagavad Gita (Mahatma Ghandi's favourite)
God talks with Arunja: the Bagavad Gita by Paramahansa Yogananda
www.gita-society.com
Hindu wisdom for all Gods children by Francis Clooney.
The Dalai Lama
How to Practice: the way to a meaningful life.
Ethics for the New Millennia.

Meditation

Mindfulness in Plain English by Henepola Gunaratana.
How to meditate, by John Novak.
Meditation for dummies, by Stephen Bodian.
The stages of meditation, by the Dalai Lama.
Concentration and Meditation by Christmas Humphries.
The idiots guide to meditation, by Jeff Davidson
www.meditationcentre.com
www.kadampa.com
www.wildmind.com

Books and authors

The road less travelled, Scott Peck.
Return to love, Marianne Williamson.
The Power of One, Bruce Courtenay.
The History of Mr Polly, HG Wells.

Destructive emotion, the Dalai Lama.
The Art Of happiness, the Dalai Lama.
Meditations, Marcus Aurelius, Emperor of Rome.

Time management

How to get control of your time and your life, by Dan Lakein.
Time tactics of very successful people, by B. Eugene Griessman.
The time trap, by R. Alec MacKenzie.
www.timemanagementguide.com
www.worldwidelearn.com

Assertion

Asserting yourself by Sharon and Gordon Bower.
Your Perfect Right by Robert Alberti and Michael Emmons.
Self Confidence
The Ultimate Secrets of Total Self Confidence by R Anthony.
How to Develop Self Confidence and Influence People by Dale Carnegie.

Self Esteem

Self Esteem by Mathew McKay and Patrick Fanning.
The Self matters Companion by Philip McGraw.

Gabriel Deeds

Rudyard Kipling's poem "If", always touches the heart of things. It is more of a creed than a mere poem. It is the culmination of a life times experience and wisdom. Many religions are founded on far less.

If

If you can keep your head when all about you,
Are losing theirs and blaming it on you,
If you can trust yourself when all men doubt you,
But make allowance for their doubting too,
If you can wait and not be tired by waiting,
Or being lied about, don't deal in lies,
Or being hated, don't give way to hating,
And yet don't look too good, nor talk too wise
If you can dream and not make dreams your master,
If you can think and not make thoughts your aim,
If you can meet with triumph and disaster,
And treat those two impostors just the same,
If you can bear to hear the truth you've spoken,
Twisted by knaves to make a trap for fools,
Or watch the things you gave your life to, broken,
And stoop and build 'em up again with worn out tools,
If you can make one heap of all your winnings,
And risk it all on one turn of pitch and toss,
And lose, and start again at your beginnings,
And never breathe a word about your loss,
If you can force your heart and nerve and sinew,
To serve your turn long after they are gone,
And so hold on when there is nothing in you,
Except the will which says to them, "Hold on!"
If you can walk with crowds and keep your virtue,
Or walk with Kings nor lose the common touch,
If neither foes nor loving friends can hurt you,
If all men count with you, but none too much,
If you can fill the unforgiving minute,
With sixty seconds worth of distance run,
Yours is the earth and everything that's in it,
And which is more, you'll be a Man my son.

Appendix 2   Movies

Matrix, life is an illusion that must be shattered.
Fight Club, we are always looking for someone to follow. The search for Self can be dangerous when we get it wrong.
The Defiant Ones, (Curtis and Poitier), we are all alike, dependent on each other.
Jerry Maguire, what matters the most? What is success?
American beauty, it's never too late, become what you are
Falling Down, how much suffering can you handle?
Awakening, there are worse things than death.
The Mission, you can be beaten but never defeated.
Ice Cold In Alex, never give in.
Cool Hand Luke, you can find victory in the strangest places.
Barney, rediscover the innocence of the child within.
Bugs Life, bullies must be fought regardless of the cost.
Tom Brown's Schooldays, the Hive always attacks the child.
Lord Of The Rings, we are all ring bearers.
The Dead poets Society, make your life extraordinary.
Clockwise, the Universe sees our plans and laughs.
Billy Elliot, the individual against family and tribe.
Moby Dick, (Gregory Peck), don't waste your life being distracted by goals, (revenge).
Remains of the day, a life of dedication and devotion, wasted.
Good will Hunting, don't hide, be the best that you can be
Educating Rita, you can be whatever you want to be.
Shadowlands, it is better to have taken the big risk and seemingly failed than hide.
The Game, death can put things into perspective.
Meet Joe Black, death comes to us all.
Sixth Sense, things are seldom what they seem.
City Of Angels
What Dreams May Come, contemplate your next ten thousand years.
Hurly Burly, escapism.
Human Traffic, illusion.
Trainspotting, suffering.

Gabriel Deeds

Saving Private Ryan, the futility of war.
Gallipoli, dulce et decorum est.
The Killing Fields, civilisation is only skin deep.
All Quiet On The Western Front, love through suffering.
Ghandi, a person inspired by belief is unstoppable.
A Man For All Seasons, sometimes it is necessary to stand up for your beliefs.
Pay It Forward, someone has to make the first move.

ISBN 1-41201737-8